Theology—Descent into
the Vicious Circles of Death

Theology—Descent into the Vicious Circles of Death

On the Fortieth Anniversary
of Jürgen Moltmann's
The Crucified God

EDITED BY ZORAN GROZDANOV

Foreword by Miroslav Volf

CASCADE *Books* • Eugene, Oregon

THEOLOGY—DESCENT INTO THE VICIOUS CIRCLES OF DEATH
On the Fortieth Anniversary of Jürgen Moltmann's *The Crucified God*

Copyright © 2016 Wipf and Stock Publishers. All rights reserved. Except for brief quotations in critical publications or reviews, no part of this book may be reproduced in any manner without prior written permission from the publisher. Write: Permissions, Wipf and Stock Publishers, 199 W. 8th Ave., Suite 3, Eugene, OR 97401.

Cascacde Books
An Imprint of Wipf and Stock Publishers
199 W. 8th Ave., Suite 3
Eugene, OR 97401

www.wipfandstock.com

PAPERBACK ISBN: 978-1-4982-3275-3
HARDCOVER ISBN: 978-1-4982-3277-7
EBOOK ISBN: 978-1-4982-3276-0

Cataloguing-in-Publication data:

Names: Grozdanov, Zoran, editor. | Volf, Miroslav, foreword.

Title: Theology—descent into the vicious circles of death : on the fortieth anniversary of Jürgen Moltmann's The Crucified God / edited by Zoran Grozdanov ; foreword by Miroslav Volf.

Description: Eugene, OR : Cascade Books, 2016 | Includes bibliographical references and index.

Identifiers: ISBN 978-1-4982-3275-3 (paperback) | ISBN 978-1-4982-3277-7 (hardcover) | ISBN 978-1-4982-3276-0 (ebook)

Subjects: LCSH: Moltmann, Jürgen. | Moltmann, Jürgen. Gekreuzigte Gott.

Classification: BT202.M553 T48 2016 (paperback) | BT202.M553 T48 (ebook)

Manufactured in the U.S.A.   12/13/16

Contents

Permissions | vii
Contributors | ix
Foreword to the U.S. Edition by Miroslav Volf | xi
Introduction | xv
—Zoran Grozdanov

1 ***The Crucified God* in Context** | 1
 —Jürgen Moltmann
 My Personal Context | 3
 The Contexts of the Impact of *The Crucified God* | 9

2 **Theology Out of Concrete Events** | 19
 —Zoran Grozdanov
 Introduction | 19
 Where Is God? The Essential Impetus of Moltmann's Theology | 24
 Atheism as a Context for the Talk of God | 25
 Metaphysics Out of Suffering? | 35
 The Outcast Nature of Revelation and Conditions of the Possibility
 of Its Realization | 41

3 The Development of Democratic Political Culture: Religions as Agents of Political Liberation? (Contextual Discussion drawing on *The Crucified God*, by J. Moltmann) | 45
—ALEN KRISTIĆ

    Introduction | 46
    I. The Burden of Nondemocratic Political Culture | 54
    II. Socialization of Nondemocratic Political Culture | 60
    III. Postmetaphysical Turnaround of Religious Sphere | 70
    IV. Contextual Implementation of the Fundamental Program of *The Crucified God* | 78

4 Theological Discourse in the Vicious Circle of Apathy | 87
—ENTONI ŠEPERIĆ

    Introduction | 87
    Jürgen Moltmann: Theology as a Biography | 88
    Theology out of the Vicious Circle of Death | 91
    Jesus's Descent into Hell | 98
    A Thing Is a Thing, and Not What Is Said (of That Thing) | 104
    Getting Hell out of Here | 107
    Conclusion | 114

5 The Pretense Veil of Christian Vulgarism: Ethno-religious Wraith in Contemporary Secular Society | 117
—BRANKO SEKULIĆ

    Boastful *depositum fidei* of Religionism | 118
    Political Religion: The History of the Disease and an Ethno-religious Diagnosis | 120
    One Flew over the Ethno-religious Nest | 123
    The Autopsy of the Ethno-religious Political Worship | 134

Index | 139

Permissions

Scriptures taken from the Holy Bible, New International Version®, NIV®. Copyright © 1973, 1978, 1984, 2011 by Biblica, Inc.™ Used by permission of Zondervan. All rights reserved worldwide. www.zondervan.com The "NIV" and "New International Version" are trademarks registered in the United States Patent and Trademark Office by Biblica, Inc.™

Jürgen Moltmann, *The Crucified God*, SCM Press 2001 © Jürgen Moltmann, 2001. Used by permission of Hymns Ancient & Modern Ltd.

Thirty brief quotes as submitted (1950 words) from *The Crucified God* by Jürgen Moltmann. English translation copyright © 1974 by SCM Press Ltd. Reprinted by permission of HarperCollins Publishers.

Contributors

Zoran Grozdanov PhD is lecturer at the Faculty of Theology Matthias Flacius Illyricus, University of Zagreb, Croatia. His publications include *Bog pred križem: zbornik u čast Jürgena Moltmana* (God in Front of the Cross: Essays in Honour of Jürgen Moltmann; 2007), and with Regina Ammicht-et al., eds., *Religion and Identity in Post-conflict Societies*, International Journal of Theology *Concilium* 1 (2015).

Alen Kristić is a theologian, translator and peace activist. Recently he has published *Tiranija religijskog: ogledi o religijskom bezboštvu* (The Tyranny of the Religious: Essays of Religious Atheism; 2014); and *Prognani u zaborav: fragmenti o pozitivnom potencijalu religioznog* (Banished into Oblivion: Forgotten Fragments of the Positive Potential of the Religious; 2015).

Jürgen Moltmann is Professor of Theology Emeritus at the University of Tübingen, Germany. Among his many awarded books, his publications include seminal *Theology of Hope* (1964), *The Crucified God* (1972), and *The Church in the Power of the Spirit* (1975).

Branko Sekulić is a PhD candidate at the Ludwig Maximilian University in Munich, Germany. He has published articles in Croatian journals (*Nova prisutnost, Autsajderski fragmenti*) and writes for Croatian independent online magazines (H-Alter, Kriz zivota, Forum.tm).

Entoni Šeperić is a PhD candidate in the Department of Philosophy, Faculty of Humanities and Social Sciences, University of

Contributors

Zagreb, Croatia, with a thesis on "St. Paul in the Political Project of the European New Left."

Foreword to the U.S. Edition

WHEN JÜRGEN MOLTMANN'S AMERICAN publisher, Fortress Press, was bringing out the fortieth-anniversary edition of *The Crucified God*, the editors asked me to write a foreword. As his former student, one who did two dissertations under his supervision—a ThD dissertation and habilitation—I was happy to oblige. In the second-to-last paragraph of that foreword I wrote,

> *The Crucified God* is theology at its best. I know some experts will complain about the inadequacies of the book's account of the mystery of the holy Trinity. Moltmann addressed some of them in subsequent work. Many of his colleagues remain unpersuaded, of course, but facing contestations is in the job description of an academic theologian. Whatever one decides about the merits and demerits of Moltmann's doctrine of the Trinity in this text, the fact remains: *The Crucified God* is a truly great book. It is existential and academic, pastoral and political, innovative and traditional, readable and demanding, contextual and universal, deeply Christian and equally deeply human—and all of this in explicating the bearing of the central Christian theme (the crucifixion of Jesus of Nazareth) on a fundamental human experience (suffering).

Moltmann himself considers *The Crucified God* his most important theological work. *Theology of Hope*, another possible candidate, had provided some key formal categories that he continued to employ in an altered form—the "promise" acquired increasingly a dimension of "presence," for instance. But *The Crucified God* laid the Trinitarian and soteriological foundation for subsequent books, starting with *The Trinity and the Kingdom*. It introduced the notion of a God who suffers in solidarity with afflicted creatures and redeems them through that suffering. This simple and profound thought lies at the heart of the book—difficult and unacceptable to many, especially among trained theologians committed to God's impassibility, but hopeful and comforting to many more, especially among the afflicted, whether they live in fear in wartorn cities, eke out a miserable existence in shantytowns, wait for death in the belly of cruel prisons, or struggle against an illness eating away at their body or soul.

Many people have recognized the greatness of Moltmann's masterpiece. It captures the heart as well as the mind, and it has done so in Asia and South America no less than in North America and his native Europe. No theologian working in the second half of the twentieth century has had as powerful a global resonance as has Moltmann.

Teologija: silazak u vražje krugove smrti (first Croatian edition, 2014), published almost half a century after *The Crucified God* (1972), shows that Moltmann's book has continued relevance today in a very different setting—political, ideological, economic, religious—than the one in which he originally wrote it: in Western Europe after student revolts, after decolonization, after the economic boom of the fifties and sixties, after the ravages of World War II, including the humiliation of Germany as a result of what the Germans did during the war (Auschwitz!) and what they suffered toward the end of it. The authors of the present book all grew up after 1989, when the rivalry on the world stage ended between two major projects of globalization, two ways of living in the world seen as a single, integrated reality. The communist project of globalization lost—definitively, I think; the capitalist project won, for now. In places like the former Yugoslavia, especially in Sarajevo, from which some of the authors come, that victory was bitter. Communist ideology gave way to the merger of religious and national ideologies, authoritarian forms of government

Foreword to the U.S. Edition

remained (often with the same political actors who overnight had undergone a political "conversion"), and widespread corruption in the processes of transition to a free market economy enriched a few and left many others destitute. On top of that, the region was plunged into a three-way war between Catholic Croatians, Muslim Bosniaks, and Orthodox Serbians, the majority of whom were religious less by conviction than by ethnic belonging. The conflict took a heavy toll: millions of refugees, hundreds of thousands of dead, many ethnically cleansed villages and towns—in a word, the suffering was immense.

Like Moltmann, the authors of this book are faced with the question, where is God when the world falls apart? Like Moltmann, they are convinced that solidarity with victims is the key both to where God is when people suffer and where we ourselves should be. Like Moltmann, they believe that both politics and religion—so closely intertwined in the Balkans—must be called into question and recast in the light of God's entry into the devilish circles of death. *Teologija: silazak u vražje krugove smrti* isn't just a wonderful tribute to the fecundity of Moltmann's thought, however. It is a contribution in its own right to living in the multiple conflicts of today, in a globalized world marked by contending particular universalisms that often turn violent.

Miroslav Volf
Henry B. Wright Professor of Theology
Founder and Director of the Yale Center for Faith and Culture

Introduction

—Zoran Grozdanov

The research and the texts contained in this book explore the possibility of materialization and concretization in the former Yugoslav region of some of Moltmann's central insights tackled in his work *The Crucified God: The Cross of Christ as the Foundation and Criticism of Christian Theology*, originally published in 1972. The idea of publishing this volume has been guided by our wish to mark, though belatedly, the fortieth anniversary of the publication of this seminal work. To that end, we have invited Prof. Moltmann and several junior theologians to take part in the *development of a (regional) contextual theology*, as it (though rather presumptuously) might be called.

Why do we take Moltmann's thought as a starting point? *The Crucified God* in particular, along with his initial work *Theology of Hope*, is widely regarded as a highly influential driving force inspiring and informing theological movements around the world, including movements that took up certain theological insights with such concreteness and seriousness that they applied them both in their sociopolitical milieu as well as in the church sphere. These latter movements, in particular, are the focus of our attention in this volume. Arguably some of the best known among them are Latin American liberation theology and, in the United States, black theology. The main concerns shared by these movements included social, political, and religious oppression and marginalization, along with the desire for transformation of social but also religious situations through those very *theological insights*. Here I specifically underscore the *theological insights* since, as opposed to our former Yugoslav and now current transitional context in which theology has never been construed as a transforming power geared toward humanization of all sociopolitical spheres, these movements adopted the central insights of Moltmann's theology: namely, from *Theology of Hope*, the insight that the eschatology, the future of God, is found in the heart of Christian theology; and from *The Crucified God*, the insight that this future is materialized on the cross, with all its religious, social, and political ramifications.

If we were to ask Mr. Moltmann whether, in writing these two books, he had had any idea of their potential influence, the answer would most likely be no. Moltmann simply seemed to wish to write books discussing theology from two foci—the resurrection and the cross, the very foundations of Christian faith—all the while referring to the moments of crisis in his own life. Now, let us consider the *kairos* of these books: the 1960s and 1970s, marked by high hopes for change in social, political, and religious structures, and the shattering of those hopes by the end of the 1960s and early 1970s, which is clearly reflected in the main themes of these books—the theology of hope inspiring hope in those who wanted change, and the theology of the cross drawing attention to the fact that the transforming power and hope unconditionally arise from *the night of the cross* with solidary *descent into the devil's circles of death*, as we have named our rather brief volume. Hope and *the newness* are inextricably linked with the *weakening* or with the hazardous transformation of own identity through the destruction of all idols of religion, nation, and society, as Moltmann calls it. In other words, the transforming power can only come through the cross as a concrete historical event bringing about concrete sociopolitical and religious causes, the cross that puts those marginalized in society, religion, and the political sphere at center stage and the place of emerging hope, transformation, and fulfillment of God's promise of righteousness.

Zoran Grozdanov   *Introduction*

We may as well here invoke the words of Jon Sobrino, one of the best-known liberation theologian, who wrote his most important works under the profound influence of Moltmann and who, in a strong Moltmannian vein, urges us to conceive of and practice theology as a reflection of daring to live *here and now*, as if we have already risen: "Christian existence is a life lived in community with the crucified, so as to take them down from the cross, since we are to live already as risen and walk—whilst standing in humility in the face of the ignominiousness of such and suchlike history—together with God, the God of the poor and the victims." Since for theology, as for any other materialization of religious existence, there is ultimately only one pressing question, that is, is it to be a perilous endeavor of taking others down from the cross—or even preventing crucifixion from ever occurring—or perhaps an ungodly process of making crosses and pinning others to them so as to appease our unease over escaping our own cross, which represents, as Moltmann rightly understands it in an utterly demystified way, two at once: everyday life and the very human existence? Perhaps it is due to its vulnerability and fragility that this existence is only worthy of even, as Christians believe, being the irrevocable selection of God himself in incarnation. This question, though not the only one, but pivotal nevertheless, arises in all theological endeavors and pretensions on religious existence in our region.

Jürgen Moltmann wrote an essay exclusively for this volume providing a very succinct description of the background to *The Crucified God*, including the backgrounds to the societies and theologies substantially informed by this book. As for his personal background, of vital importance were his war experience in the Antiaircraft Defense in Hamburg during Operation Gomorrah in 1943, and the demise of his best friend in that battle. That was the first time, as referred to in his text and his memories in *A Broad Place* (*Weiter Raum*, 2006), Moltmann posed the question underlying his entire theology: *Where is God* in the midst of all suffering and death? Moltmann found the answer to this question, which is central not only to *The Crucified God* but to his entire work, in the cross, with all its historical but also social, political, and religious causes, as well as in all the theological implications stemming from the cross.

The second essay, titled "Theology Out of Concrete Events," written by Zoran Grozdanov, explores the potential for materialization and reassessment of conditions for the possibility of seeing *The Crucified God* as a groundwork for the development of theology out of a concrete historical event. The concreteness of the cross of Jesus and the concreteness of God's revelation are an essential requirement for possible development of Moltmann's theology, which does not take as a starting point a God who is an objective given, but a God whose character can be understood entirely through Jesus's conflicts with the society and religion of his time, as well as through the godforsakenness of the cross in Jesus's death cry, "My *God*, my *God*, why hast thou *forsaken me*?"

The concreteness of the cross and its ramifications in terms of the sociopolitical and religious context of our post-Yugoslav region are the main thrust of research presented by Alen Kristić, Branko Sekulić, and Entoni Šeperić.

Pointing up the common ground between Moltmann's theology and the "weak Christianity" espoused by philosopher G. Vattimo, Alen Kristić claims that the fundamental core of Moltmann's theological project at the other side of *metaphyiscal mentality* represents *the solidary descent into the devil's circles of death of our own time and space*. This is, in fact, the unconditional criterion of authenticity not only of theology, but also of Christian as well as religious existence in general—the struggle for humanization of society in all its aspects through solidary union with the people whose human dignity is threatened. Providing a local-level assessment of mechanisms in place in regional religious communities which prevent the "solidary descent into the concrete devil's circles of death," Kristić finds that for religions in Bosnia and Herzegovina, and in the Balkan region generally, the contextualized implementation of the fundamental program of Moltmann's *Crucified God*, primarily meant as a kenotic solidary descent of religions in the current situations of crucified God or current devil's circles of death, entails a kenotic and solidary departure away from utopias of nationalistic and religious ghettos and toward heterotopias of postwar transitional traumas.

Entoni Šeperić ponders the constitutive deafness and apathy of the contemporary theological discourse, expounding on the article of the Apostles' Creed on Jesus's descent into hell—or, rather more precisely, on a theological dispute over the orthodoxy of its interpretation in the theology of Hans Urs von Balthasar. Making a critical correlation with the texts of Moltmann and Metz, it strives to reflect on the limitations and difficulties stemming from the theological idealism and the inescapability of contextual reflection on theology out of the devil's circle of apathy of the theological discourse. It provides an unfaltering insight into the futility of the ideological concept of orthodoxy as the logic of conceiving Christian certainties, as well as the possibility of responding to the factuality of mass murders and genocides with the cold disinterestedness of academic theology, now seemingly absorbed in nothing else save the formal criterion of orthodoxy as its own standard.

The final essay in the volume, titled "The Pretense Veil of Christian Vulgarism: Ethno-religious Wraith in Contemporary Secular Society," written by Branko Sekulić, deals with the issue of the intertwining of religious, political, and ethnic matters, summed up by the author in a catch-all term: *ethno-religionism*. In his interpretation of Moltmann's central insights into the potential for the political liberation of an individual, including liberation of religious communities and the church from politics, the author warns that, in our context, the church no longer seems to provide an authentic meaning of a single faith-worshipping context, but rather a primitive mask laden with interests of highly-charged politicking, while its main impetus, instead of being an eschatological dimension of hope of the living God, is now reduced to the incessant digging up and over the burial grounds of the crucified one. For the church, his materialization marks the end of mythological manipulations whereupon it builds its foundations in the context of ethnic differentiation. To such church, the author argues, the cross is good enough only as a symbol scribbled on tombstones, and in no way as a symbol of resurrection and an urgent need for radical spiritual challenges. Thus the church in this variant comes out as an apparition only to be accessed by way of certain pathological theological instruments. As a result, in order for it to realize its existence in the context of Christ's message of the fight for life, it should first of all get out of his grave and grant that he is alive indeed.

The main objective of this volume is to try to make theology truly regarded as an area of human research, interest, and belief that can positively shape and inform the reality we live in—the reality of an individual as well as the reality of a religious community and the society in general. In other words, "for the theologians the matter is not to provide a different interpretation of the world, the history and human being, but for *them* to be transformed in expectation of a divine transformation" (Moltmann).

1

The Crucified God in Context

—Jürgen Moltmann

When *The Crucified God* was published in 1972, it sparked an intense and very controversial international theological discussion about this radical theory of the cross. Michael Welker edited a collection of first reactions in *Diskussion über Jürgen Moltmanns Buch "Der gekreuzigte Gott"* (Munich, 1979). Later, numerous dissertations, articles, and books followed, dealing with various theological questions that *The Crucified God* had raised. Today, forty years later, instead of discussing the theological contents, I would like to present the hermeneutical contexts that may give a better understanding of the book. I will do this by putting myself back, as best I can, into my own situation that led me to write the book, as well as understanding the situations of those who received it because of their own personal experiences. I will begin with my personal, original context and will then discuss the contexts within which the book has had an impact. Every text's *context* also has its *kairos* and its *community*. These are the three basic elements of any realistic hermeneutic.

Theology—Descent into the Vicious Circles of Death

What are the personal life-and-death experiences that influenced the writing of *The Crucified God*?

> Since I first studied theology, I have been concerned with the theology of the cross. . . . This no doubt goes back to the period of my first concern with questions of Christian faith and theology in actual life, as a prisoner of war behind barbed wire. . . . Shattered and broken, the survivors of my generation were then returning from camps and hospitals to the lecture room. A theology which did not speak of God in the sight of the one who was abandoned and crucified would have had nothing to say to us then.[1]

So I wrote in the book's introduction.

In discussions, I have easily admitted that I poured my heart and soul into writing this book. My personal experiences of death and forsakenness led me to the divine mystery of the forsaken, suffering, and dying Jesus. The burdens and traumas of my "generation of 1945" in wartime Germany and Auschwitz were the broader context for this theology of the cross, which goes beyond a doctrine of salvation and reaches the apocalyptic horizons of the world.

The picture I had on my desk as I was thinking about and writing the book was Marc Chagall's *Crucifixion in Yellow*.

> It shows the figure of the crucified Christ in an apocalyptic situation: people sinking into the sea, people homeless and in flight, and yellow fire blazing in the background. And with the crucified Christ there appears the angel with the trumpet and the open roll of the book of life. This picture has accompanied me for a long time. It symbolizes the cross on the horizon of the world, and can be thought of as a symbolic expression of the studies which follow.[2]

This is what I wrote at the end of the introduction.

---

1. Moltmann, *Crucified God*, 1.
2. Ibid., 6.

MY PERSONAL CONTEXT

My Lost Youth

More than five years of my youth, from the age of sixteen to twenty-two, from 1943 to 1948, were senselessly wasted—from an outsider's perspective. I survived bomb attacks, endured among the dying and the dead, doing forced labor in prison camps. These experiences with death had a profound impact on me. Just as I was discovering the sciences and poetry, I was drafted into the Wehrmacht, in 1943; in the English POW camps I was considered a "baby prisoner." Even after I was physically released from captivity in April 1948, my soul remained in bondage for a long time. Even today, I still feel the scars of my wounded soul. When I remember these things that are locked away, hidden deeply in the abysses of my memories, they are still so very present, as if they were happening now.

The Betrayed Generation

At the end of July 1943, the English Royal Air Force bombed my hometown, Hamburg. The devastation of the first German city was called Operation Gomorrah. Forty thousand people died in the firestorm, mostly women and children because the men were fighting on the front. I miraculously survived the inferno. We were convinced that the war was over since the Luftwaffe had already been almost completely destroyed. Even though Germany had already lost the war it had started, Hitler and the Nazis wanted to take the German people down with them. In the senseless battles from 1943 to 1945, millions more died, millions were murdered, and a campaign of indescribable destruction was carried out. Paul Celan wrote, "Death is a master from Germany." To continue to wage a war that was already lost was nothing less than mass murder, an orgy of death, and a perverse desire to destroy life. In the prison camps I had three years to mentally and emotionally process all these experiences of death, and to find the desire to live once again. I was not able to simply throw myself into rebuilding the country, oblivious to everything that had happened, as the people in postwar Germany did. Night after night, the horrors overcame and tortured me until, reading the Bible, I found the crucified Christ who carried my fears and anguish with me. This faith had saved me.

The Generation of Perpetrators

I belong to the "generation of 1945" in Germany. When, in 1945, while in a prison camp in Scotland, we were shown pictures of the concentration camps of Bergen-Belsen, Buchenwald, and Auschwitz, I understood that fate had—against my will—made me a member of the generation of perpetrators. I had to bear the shame of the mass murder of the Jews. I had not participated personally, but we were collectively responsible for the thousands of starving Russian prisoners in German prison camps, for the hostage executions in the partisan war, for the "scorched earth" policy, and many more war crimes. In 1961 I walked through what was left of the death camp Majdanek, near Lublin. I saw the children's shoes, the cut off hair, and I was overwhelmed by shame. And as I walked alone through one of the camp's streets I had a vision: I saw the murdered children walking toward me in the fog. Since then, I have been convinced that there is a resurrection of the dead.

I know what it means to belong to the "nation of perpetrators." For me, the "sacred fatherland" of the Germans ceased to exist and any feelings of patriotism had died. I was ready to bear the shame of my people, to admit the guilt of my people, as proclaimed in the Stuttgart Declaration of Guilt (*Stuttgarter Schuldbekenntnis*) issued in 1945 by the Council of the Evagelical Church in Germany; I was prepared to work toward repentance among the people by admitting the truth, converting hearts, and making reparations, as far as this is even possible. However, I felt at home as a Christian in the worldwide Christian church. Germany was merely the place where providence had placed me; it had not been my choice. At that time, I could not get the phrase from the early

Letter to Diognetus out of my mind: "Every foreign country is a fatherland to them, and every fatherland is foreign."

The following generations do not have to bear the shame anymore. Yet they must understand their responsibility based on their relationship with the war generation. The "mercy of a late birth," as Chancellor Helmut Kohl claimed for himself, does not exist.

What had I experienced? Were these the crimes of an "unjust war"? Were they deplorable war crimes? I struggled to find moral terms and theological concepts: Was it the power of sin? Was it radical evil? Was it the iniquity of the godless? Was it the curse of God in the abyss of death? Was it the hell of the condemned? Surely it was all of these. However, I still could not find a concept that made it possible to comprehend that which was so horrendous and unfathomable. Elie Wiesel once said, "One cannot understand Auschwitz either without God or with God."

The dying Christ was a "comfort" to me because he himself had died with open, unanswered questions. "My God, why have you forsaken me?" When he died on the cross, according to the gospels, darkness came over the whole land and the curtain in the temple was torn in two (Luke 23:44–45). This is a symbolic expression of the "eclipse of God," as Martin Buber describes this apocalyptic hour. This helped me to recognize my own experiences in the situation of the dying Christ, to endure the incomprehensible, and live with the unanswered questions. The key experience for being able to understand—no, for being able to bear—the horrors I had survived was Christ being forsaken by God. For me, this is the apocalyptic dimension of the passion of Christ. For this reason, the renewed discussions about the interpretation of the death of Christ as the atonement for "our sins" seems petty and ignorant to me. No traditional concept of sin, not even the seven mortal sins, can adequately deal with these horrors. Paul even says that Christ was cursed by God: "He became a curse for us" (Gal 3:13). Only someone who has suffered the curse of God—whether as a victim or as a perpetrator—can understand this. This is one of the reasons why *The Crucified God* has been labeled the first German book of theology "after Auschwitz": Jesus was murdered in Auschwitz. He died in the gas chambers. Jesus was tortured in Argentina. Jesus died on the lynching tree in the United States. Jesus was shot in Srebrenica. Wherever people are murdered, gassed, tortured, or shot, the Crucified is among them. He belongs to them; they are his brothers and sisters. They are his people. They partake in his passion.

Shattered Hopes

While I was writing *Theology of Hope*, deep down inside I already felt compelled by the theology of the cross. But I was not yet ready to deal with these difficult questions. In the book *Diskussion über die "Theologie der Hoffnung,"* which Wolf-Dieter Marsch published in 1967, I had already written something about the God of the future and the crucified Christ in answer to the "unusually intense and varied responses"[3] the book had provoked. However, I did not make the decision to write this book and to give it its harsh title until the fateful year 1968. When I refer to the year 1968, I am not referring to the revolutionary "generation of 1968," but to the violent way in which the hopes of that generation, which had led to those new beginnings and movements, one of which was also my *Theology of Hope*, were violently shattered.

In 1967–68 I was at Duke University, in Durham, North Carolina, as a guest lecturer for a semester. The English translation of my book *Theology of Hope* had been published in 1967. In the United States, the civil rights movement had embraced it wholeheartedly. Before I left, the divinity school organized a nationwide conference about the book. All the important names in theology had come. On the second day, while I was just discussing the difference between the English term *history* and the German term *Geschichte*, Harvey Cox stormed into the hall and shouted, "Martin Luther King has been shot!" It was April 4, 1968. We watched on television as the justified fury of the Blacks, as the Afro-Americans were referred to back then, unleashed itself in riots and fires.

---

3. Cf. Marsch, *Diskussion über die "Theologie der Hoffnung,"* 222–29.

The conference ended abruptly. The participants rushed home. A curfew was enforced in Durham. The prophet of the civil rights movement had been murdered and with him his dream of a "beloved community" in which people would no longer be judged by the color of their skin but by their character. However, this murder did not stop the civil rights movement. That evening, we sang defiantly with the students, "We shall overcome . . ." But it was clear to us that there was no hope of liberation from racism and violence without the cross and being disciples of the Crucified.

When I returned to Tübingen and was holding my first lectures, there was an assassination attempt on student leader Rudi Dutschke in Berlin. He later died from the long-term effects of the gunshot wound to his head. Before that, the student Benno Ohnesorg had been shot by police in Berlin. It was the end of the peaceful, nonviolent protests. The violence of death had taken over and was reigning.

In the middle of the Stalinist Eastern bloc, a new "socialism with a human face" appeared with Alexander Dubček. And with him, a new spirit emerged in a Europe divided by the Cold War: the propaganda wars in the East and West were replaced by "dialogue." The Catholic Paulusgesellschaft organized the highly acclaimed Christian-Marxist dialogues in Herrenchiemsee in 1966, in Innsbruck in 1967, and in Mariánské Lázně (Marienbad), in Czechoslovakia, in 1968. The driving force was the Czech philosopher Milan Machovec; the encounter was inspired by Ernst Bloch; Karl Rahner and Roger Garaudy represented the new openness of Christians and Marxists toward each other. I was present in Marienbad with my friend John Baptist Metz. We were promoting a new political theology. The Czech philosophers, however, wanted to learn about the new transcendence from the Christian theologians—a transcendence that does not alienate but that liberates. It was a memorable conference in May 1968. In the East and in the West, we were convinced that a united European peace process was possible.

And then it all came to an abrupt end in August 1968: Warsaw Pact tanks rolled into Czechoslovakia and brutally crushed the "human face" of socialism. Our Marxist colleagues were arrested, Machovec was robbed of every source of livelihood, Gardavsky died after incessant interrogations, Prucha and others fled to the West. And now the lights are shutting down in Prague for twenty years, I predicted at the time; it took twenty-one years for Stalinist terror to disappear from Russia and Eastern Europe. That fall, in 1968, I was paralyzed for months. In the former GDR, my books were no longer allowed to be distributed and my name was not allowed to be mentioned. I had been placed on the blacklist as a "convergence theorist, a CIA agent, and an anarchist." *Theology of Hope* was confiscated at the border to the GDR. In this situation, I could only maintain the theology of hope as a theology of the cross.

I would like to mention one more change in the worldwide context: in the year 1968, the Vatican published the encyclical *Humanae Vitae*, the so-called pill encyclical. This was the sign that the conservative forces within the Catholic Church and the Vatican were stopping the enormous impact of the Second Vatican Council.

In 1962 no one could have imagined that the Roman Catholic Church, which had been on the defensive since the French Revolution, would change under Pope John XXIII in the spirit of *aggiornamento*, opening itself to the modern world and to ecumenism. This miracle had taken place in only three short years, from 1962 to 1965. Other churches were envious of the Catholic Church for the courageous steps it had taken with the Second Vatican Council. Protestant theologians were regular guests in Rome and interacted in an atmosphere of mutual understanding, respect, and harmony. And then this encyclical, forbidding birth control, was issued. Very few had seen it coming.

Catholic moral theologians who decided differently had their ecclesiastical right to teach (*missio canonica*) revoked; Protestant theologians who advocated responsible parenthood were rejected. The ecumenical community, once again, had a stumbling block placed in its way. Ecumenical friendships among church leaders cooled off noticeably, although at the same time they were becoming more and more normal at the grassroots level. The Ecumenical Council of Churches in Geneva celebrated a climax of hope in 1968 at the Fourth Assembly of the World Council of Churches in Uppsala with the theme "Behold, I make all things new." After the assembly, however, an ecumenical winter set in, especially in Germany. Today, my former colleague in Tübingen, Joseph Ratzinger, is generally thought to have been responsible for this.

In 1968 many hopes were shattered all over the world: in Latin America, CIA-controlled military dictatorships suppressed the people's desire for freedom and murdered thousands. In China, the crimes of Mao's Cultural Revolution became known. In the Federal Republic of Germany, the government, under Willy Brandt, unfortunately introduced emergency laws and banned communists from certain professions—although there were not very many of them.

For me, the consequence of all this was the following conclusion: Christian hope is not a kind of optimism based on positive thinking, nor is it a religion of success. It is Christian and has a divine foundation when it is based on the resurrection of the Christ who was persecuted and knows trials and temptations. It is then a hope that is born again, out of its own disappointments. It is then a force that gives strength to persevere against the forces of death and toward the victory of life.

THE CONTEXTS OF THE IMPACT OF *THE CRUCIFIED GOD*

My Personal Contexts

I will begin with the intellectual and spiritual contexts and then discuss the different cultural and political contexts.

In his preface to the SCM Classics edition of *The Crucified God*, Richard Bauckham writes that it "is undoubtedly one of the theological classics of the second half of the twentieth century. What marks it as a classic is that, when one rereads it several

Theology—Descent into the Vicious Circles of Death

decades later, themes, which were innovative in its time, seem now rather familiar . . . but also that it still shocks and surprises, enlightens and provokes, with its dialectical sharpness of expression. . . . It is a passionate book." I am not sure if Richard Bauckham is right; however, I do know that this book is a part of my wrestling with God, as it is described, suffering under the dark side of God, his hidden face, that reveals itself in the godlessness of the perpetrators and the godforsakenness of the victims in the human history of injustice and violence. The connection between experience and reflection may be one of the reasons why the book has been published numerous times in many countries since 1972. The dialectical sharpness of expression may have spurred the many theological discussions. Yet it is my personal experience that has brought me the many letters from monasteries, prisons, and hospitals, from people who are suffering and wrestling with God. One woman wrote to tell me how the book had reached out and touched her in the "dark night" of her soul. A man, a theologian, told how the book kept him from committing suicide. I am currently corresponding with a woman who is reading the book while on death row in America, where she has been waiting to be executed for twelve years. I would never have thought that a book on theology could reach so many people in their personal struggles. It certainly is not an easy book to read, and it was not written with any pastoral intent.

I felt a special bond with Pope John Paul II based on the spirituality of the cross. On Christmas Day 2003, apparently a shadow of apocalyptic darkness fell in Saint Peter's in Rome. Pope John Paul II suddenly and unexpectedly saw the night of godforsakenness fall over our world. He was personally very shaken by this terrifying vision. He said to the pilgrims, "Besides the sword and hunger, there is an even greater tragedy: It is the silence of God, who does not reveal himself anymore, who seems to have locked himself into his heaven, disgusted by human behavior. So we now feel alone and abandoned, without peace, without salvation, without hope. The people, that have been left to fend for themselves, feel lost and overwhelmed by the horror." In Germany, even the news magazine *Der Spiegel* was shocked, and reported extensively about it. The pope referred to the prophet Jeremiah and called the people to repent: "You must recognize that your sinful behavior is the reason for the divine silence." But I asked myself, how should we repent if God has turned his back on us and is against us and not with us? Pope John Paul II always appeared with a staff with a crucifix, and as he grew older and frailer, he clearly clung to it: *A cruce regnat Deus. Ave crux, spes unica.*

This is based on the hidden spirituality of the prayer in Gethsemane. Jesus's prayer in the Garden of Gethsemane, "Let this cup pass . . ." was not answered by the Father of Jesus Christ. Jesus thus concluded that he must go the way of the cross, forsaken by his God and Father. For this reason he rebuked his sleeping disciples: "Could you not keep watch with me for one hour?" The prayer of Gethsemane means to keep watch with Jesus in the hour of godforsakenness. In Lublin, where Karol Wojtyła was professor, people remember that he would pray the Stations of the Cross every day in the quiet chapel of the Ursuline convent. He insisted that the prayer of Gethsemane had to continue and should never stop: "keeping watch with Christ" in the conflicts of the world, in the silence of God, until the day of God begins.

The Latin American Tragedy

In the same year in which *The Crucified God* was published, Gustavo Gutiérrez's famous *Teologia de la liberación* also appeared, in Spain. After several attempts with a "development theology" or a "revolution theology," this new Latin American theology finally found an adequate expression of its context and *kairos*. It was the theological implementation of the "preferential option of the poor" that had been agreed upon by the Latin American Bishops Conference in Medellín in 1968: for a "church of the poor," for a theology that serves to critically reflect its own practice, for the future of the kingdom of God, for the actual practice of liberation. At the same time, however, it was also an act of liberating Latin American theology from Europe, its center. They wanted to tap into their own sources. However, they still had a long way to go: 50 percent of the clergy in Peru was from Spain; the footnotes in *A Theology of Liberation* are all, without exception, citing European sources; the social analysis were all Marxist—and rightly so, even though this meant that liberation theology got caught in the crossfire of the Cold War between the East and the West. Because of this, foreign elements entered the Latin American context, and liberation theologians were not only persecuted by the Vatican but also by the CIA and their helpers in the various Latin American military dictatorships.

In the introduction to his book, Gutiérrez makes reference to *Theology of Hope*, and I was excited about his *A Theology of Liberation*; I was enthusiastic to partner with this new theological movement in these countries. However, in 1975, a group of theology students from Argentina and Brazil came to Tübingen to tell us that they wanted to liberate themselves from German theology; they would no longer read Barth, Bultmann, or Moltmann, because Karl Marx had said that all of history is about class struggle. They refused to answer the ironic question of where Marx had been born. I was so angry because of this that I wrote an open letter to my friend José Míguez Bonino in Buenos Aires. In it, I told him how upset I was about this "seminar Marxism" and pointed out that Stalinist Marxism was very real. In Latin America the reaction to my letter and to me was very hostile. I had not yet understood that they merely wanted to liberate themselves from intellectual colonialism.

In 1977 the World Council of Churches sent me on a big trip through Latin America. I accepted the offer, not only to give lectures at the Protestant university ISEDET in Buenos Aires but also in order to look for Elisabeth Käsemann, the daughter of my colleague Ernst Käsemann, who had "disappeared" in the city. As a social worker, she had been helping people who were being persecuted to escape and had been kidnapped by the secret services. They severely mistreated her in the torture barracks and then shot her. Surprisingly, they turned over her body. I buried her in the summer of 1977 in Tübingen. In the fall, when I went to Buenos

Aires, the situation was close to a civil war. The German ambassador was too terrified to try to have done anything for Elisabeth Käsemann. For the government of the Federal Republic of Germany economic relations were more important than human lives. This story describes the Latin American context of *A Theology of Liberation* and of my theology of the cross very well.

In 1991 the Goethe Institute sent me on another trip through Latin America. This trip took me to, among other places, Nicaragua. In Managua there is a big evangelical seminary on the Atlantic coast for the Protestant churches. I gave lectures there and also spoke as an evangelist in a marketplace in Matagalpa. I decided to concentrate on the poorest people group in Central America. I was tired of the ivory tower ecumenical theology of conferences. After this first visit, I went to Managua every two years. I celebrated the victory of the Sandinistas over the Somoza dictatorship with the Christians there. And together, we founded the first Protestant university in the country. I have grown very fond of this nation of poets and singers and this land of volcanoes and lagoons.

In 1990 I received a letter from the American theologian Robert McAfee Brown. He had just returned from San Salvador, and he reported the following: on November 16, 1989, government soldiers murdered six Jesuit fathers at the Universidad Centroamericana. They also murdered the housekeeper and her daughter in an especially brutal manner. Their intention was to silence the critical voice of Ignacio Ellacuría, so they hacked out his brain after they killed him. We will never forget that night. Jon Sobrino, who had written his doctoral thesis on my Christology at the Sankt Georgen Graduate School in Frankfurt, happened to be out of the country at the time. When the murderers dragged some of the bodies back into the building, they took the dead body of Juan Ramón Moreno into Jon Sobrino's room. They bumped a bookshelf, and a book fell onto the floor and got soaked in the martyr's blood. When the priests picked up the book the next day, they saw that it was my book. Two years later, I went on a pilgrimage to the graves of the martyrs and found my blood-soaked book there, kept in a glass case, as a symbol of what had really taken place that murderous night. The book's text had found its Latin American context and *kairos*.

Racial Tragedy in the United States

When I came to the southern United States in 1967, the civil rights movement for equal rights for blacks and for their liberation from white racism was well underway. White and black housing areas were still segregated. There was a joke that racial integration took place when blacks moved into a street and whites moved out. The only black person I ever saw at the faculty was the janitor who took out the garbage. My friend Fred Herzog, professor at Duke University, made it a point to take me into the conflict areas. One day, we came to a church in the country. The Ku Klux Klan had burned a wooden cross in front of it in order to frighten and humiliate the blacks. That, to me, was the ultimate form of perversity I could imagine: did the Klan want to "crucify" Christ in the oppressed blacks? The church had taken the scorched cross inside and put it behind the altar. They had taken the symbol of their humiliation and turned it into the symbol of their resistance: the Crucified would be resurrected—and they together with him! This image of the scorched wooden cross in this small church in North Carolina has etched itself deep into my memory.

For two thousand years the cross has, for the Christian faith, been a symbol of the redemption from sin. And so it has been moved further and further away from the victims of injustice and violence, the ones the Crucified actually belonged to. Jesus was perceived as a divine sacrifice, but no longer as a human victim. However, as Johann Baptist Metz once ironically remarked, Christ was not crucified between two candlesticks on the altar but between two poor victims of the violence of the Roman powers who ruled Jerusalem at the time. It was high time, in the extremely violent twentieth century, for the theology of the cross to be liberated from its religious and sacramental alienation and be brought back down to the bloodstained earth. This was the purpose of *The Crucified God*.

Luther said the following about the realistic theology of the cross: *Theologia crucis dicit quod res ist.*

This is exactly what my friend, the black theologian Jim Cone, of Union Theological Seminary, New York, did for the North American context with his book *The Cross and the Lynching Tree* (2011). After the American Civil War, whites in the southern states were no longer able to maintain their dominance through slavery, so they used the lynching tree. The Klu Klux Klan murdered several thousand blacks in the cruelest ways imaginable, such as torture, hanging, mutilation, and tarring and feathering. They did this as publicly as possible and often announced their attacks in order to terrorize the black population. "Lynching was the white community's way of forcibly reminding blacks of their inferiority and powerlessness."[4] The government in Washington and the Central court approved this form of white terrorism, or deliberately looked away. The last cases of public lynching were in 1936 and 1938. "The lynching tree is a metaphor for white America's crucifixion of black people. It is the window that best reveals the religious meaning of the cross in our land."[5]

This realistic view of the crucified Christ brings us into solidarity with the victims at the lynching tree, and these victims allow us to better understand the crucified God. "The cross and the lynching tree interpret each other."[6] "Can the cross redeem the lynching tree? Can the lynching tree liberate the cross?" asks Jim Cone. And he answers, "The lynching tree can liberate the crucified Christ from false piety, but the lynching tree also needs the crucified Christ, because he reveals God's presence in the victims and brings them hope for freedom and life."

Because black slaves knew the significance of the pain and shame of Jesus's death on the cross, they found themselves by his side.

"Were you there when they crucified my Lord? . . . Were you there when they nailed him to the tree?" a spiritual asks.

4. Cone, *Cross and the Lynching Tree*, 7.
5. Ibid., 166.
6. Ibid., 161.

Jim Cone states that "if Jesus was not alone in his suffering, then they were not alone in their slavery."

> Nobody knows the trouble I've seen
> Nobody knows my sorrow.
> Nobody knows the trouble I've seen
> Nobody knows but Jesus.

This is the theology of the crucified Christ's solidarity with the tormented, and the solidarity of the tormented with the crucified God.[7]

The People of Jesus in South Korea

In 1975, when I was in South Korea for the first time, it was ruled by General Park's military dictatorship. Protesting workers and students were thrown into prison and mistreated. Mothers protested in front of the Cathedral of Seoul with black scarves. This is the situation in which the Korean *minjung* theology came into being.

It does not happen very often that an exegetical discovery leads to a new theology. In his New Testament doctoral thesis, Professor Ahn Byun-Mu studied the relationship Jesus had with the people, with the *ochlos*—not the *laos*, as the people of God are called, nor the *ethne*, as the Gentiles are called—and in the Gospel of Mark he discovered the profound interdependence between Jesus and the poor, oppressed, and despised *ochlos*. For the Korean translation, he chose the term *minjung*. This term does not refer to the Korean nation, nor to the industrial proletariat, but to the entire suffering lower class of society. It is out of this that the Korean resistance traditions were born, which erupted in revolts whenever the pain, referred to as *han*, became unbearable. "In the eyes of the forsaken, scattered, and sick *minjung*, Jesus is not the church's distant 'Christ who wears a golden crown,' but the people's brother in times of need and distress, because he has personally suffered the same fate as they have," wrote Ahn Byun-Mu. Both

---

7. Cf. Cone, *Spirituals and the Blues*.

the *minjung* and Jesus of Nazareth participate in the mission of the "suffering servant of God" in Isaiah 53, "who carries the sins of the world." Solidarity and substitution come together in *minjung* theology. The theology of the cross of the *minjung* theologians is very similar to that of *The Crucified God*. They find his presence in the humiliated *minjung* in Korea and recognize the spirit of the resurrection in the positive side of *han*, which "empowers" the poor for liberation and resurrection.[8]

—Translated by Claudia Keller-Pilsel

---

8. Cf. Moltmann, *Minjung*.

BIBLIOGRAPHY

Cone, James H. *The Cross and the Lynching Tree*. Maryknoll, NY: Orbis, 2013.
———. *The Spirituals and the Blues: An Interpretation*. New York: Seabury, 1972.
Marsch, Wolf-Dieter, ed. *Diskussion über die "Theologie der Hoffnung"*. Munich: Kaiser, 1967.
Moltmann, Jürgen. *The Crucified God: The Cross of Christ as Foundation and Criticism of Christian Theology*. Translated by R. A. Wilson and John Bowden. Minneapolis: Fortress, 1993.
———, ed. *Minjung: Theologie des Volkes Gottes in Südkorea*. Neukirchen-Vluyn: Neukirchener, 1984.
Welker, Michael, ed. *Diskussion über Jürgen Moltmanns Buch "Der gekreuzigte Gott"*. Munich: Kaiser, 1979.

2

Theology Out of Concrete Events

—Zoran Grozdanov

INTRODUCTION

THE YEAR 2012 MARKED the fortieth anniversary of the publication of *The Crucified God: The Cross of Christ as the Foundation and Criticism of Christian Theology*, one of the most influential texts not only of contemporary Protestant theology, but of Christian theology in general. Coupled with *Theology of Hope*—perhaps Moltmann's more influential work (published in 1964), but for him not more important than *The Crucified God*—the reception that *The Crucified God* had in different theologies around the world has already been widely described and elaborated. Theologies developing directly or indirectly out of the insight of these two works of Moltmann are rooted in the experiences of the people and/or individuals, members of those theologies, as set forth by Moltmann himself in the description of these influences in this volume. Mentioning just a few of those theologies will suffice for the present purposes: Minjung theology in South Korea, Black theology in

North America, and of course the best known, liberation theology of Latin America. All of them shared one common concern: the experience of the oppressed and victims who have striven to give theological expression to this cry while pursuing their freedom from racial segregation and social and class inequalities. Insights into Moltmann's theology as expounded in these two works have served as a strong foundation in this process.

Therefore, it is interesting to note that our South Slavic region never experienced the development of a Balkan-specific or an ex-Yugoslav theology, although, historically speaking, it has been more than fertile ground for the emergence of such a theology, in particular in the last sixty years.[1] In this period, the church endured an outright atheistic regime which "forcefully 'silenced' pluralities and differences more so in public than in everyday, ordinary life ... excluding religion from the sphere of social decision-making."[2] Also, although playing no part in public decision-making, it is important to point out that religion, stripped of any social, and in particular political import, found its full expression on the margins of society, and, as widely claimed, spread its message, pastorally and intellectually, far more strongly than it does today.

Furthermore, the fall of communism was followed by a bloody disintegration of the state structures of Yugoslavia where religion emerged as the "historical winner,"[3] and the stronghold of ethnic and national identity, whether it be Croatian, Serbian, or Bosniak, acquired thus not only social and political recognition and all the entitlements and privileges that go with it, but also immense social and political influence.

---

1. This paper will not discuss the reasons for failure of a specific ex-Yugoslav theology in the period between the two wars, namely the Second World War and the recent conflicts in ex-Yugoslavia. However, a very informed outline of the theological (non)reception of various insights of the political theology through Marxist thought is given in an article by Darko Đogo, entitled "Politikantska ili politička teologija 1945–2010 ili o (ne)mogućnosti jedne jugoslovenske političke teologije," in Sremac et al., *Opasna sjećanja i pomirenje*, where the main part of the text is focused on the period between the two World Wars.

2. Šarčević, "Kako preobraziti naš stari svijet," 176.

3. Ibid.

Notwithstanding the forms and worth of such influence, for the purposes of this discussion it is enough to recall all the human experiences during the conflicts in ex-Yugoslavia which could have shaped and created a specific theology that would, as Moltmann stated in the preface to the Croatian edition of *The Crucified God*, "immerse theology in the experience of people and the experience of people immerse in theology."[4] The experiences of suffering, affliction, witnessing the political and religious leaders covering up criminals, marginalization of victims belonging to opposing national or ethnic groups—all of those postwar social injustices including criminal privatization of social property have never found their place in the *theological* consideration of these realities. One of Moltmann's fundamental theological intents has never found reception or consideration in our region:

> To make the cross a present reality in our civilization means to put into practice the experience one has received of being liberated from fear for oneself; no longer to adapt oneself to this society, its idols and taboos, its imaginary enemies and fetishes; *and in the name of him who was once the victim of religion, society and the state to enter into solidarity with the victims of religion, society and the state at the present day, in the same way as he who was crucified became their brother and their liberator*.[5]

Far from being a mere admonition on such reality or, even more perniciously, an apologia of that reality, theology, according to Moltmann, is rather a change of reality from the perspective and the event of the Crucified.

The permanent state of theological silence on all of these events and experiences is all the more confusing given the fact that opportunities, at least those academic and theological ones, have for a change been plentiful, to say the least.

However, close inspection of the scope and depth of Moltmann's influence on various theological movements across the world and the study of his thought among our theologians reveals

---

4. Moltmann, *Raspeti Bog*, 8.
5. Moltmann, *Crucified God*, 36 (my emphasis).

that his work has indeed been the subject of some study and reading in our area in the last three decades.[6] However, the lack of incentive, whether historical or theological, for more substantial activity in this respect does not explain the failure of shaping a theology grounded on a concrete historical situation and concrete experiences of individuals or peoples but rather the understanding of theology that is unable to read the nature of God out of concrete events, whereby the concrete events are *absorbed* into the notion of God as an objective givenness which in these concrete events does not see the contingency and breakdown of that objective givenness and such understanding of God. In other words, we could claim that such theology is guided by shielding the divine nature of God from the concrete historical events which radically challenge such divine nature and render it redundant by failing to respond to the concrete suffering that defy any explanation by a priori knowledge on man and God.

The immersion in the theology of Jürgen Moltmann inevitably includes an encounter with his penetrating theological thought aimed at changing not only individual human circumstances and lives but also the society they live in.[7] How can theology contribute to social change without assuming an apologetic stance toward teachings and postulates that it finds absolute and relevant for the

---

6. According to my knowledge, six professors currently holding chairs at the universities of theology in Croatia wrote their doctoral theses on different aspects of Moltmann's theology, including: Dogan, Nikola. *Theologie der Offenbarung: Eine-fundamental-theologische Untersuchung zum Begriff der Offenbarung in der Theologie Jürgen Moltmanns*. Rome, 1980; Karlić, Ivan. *Il Gesú della storia nella Theologia di Jürgen Moltmann*. Rome, 1996; Mateljan, Ante. *Il pensiero soteriologico nel prima ciclo Teologico di Jürgen Moltmann*. Rome, 1991; Matič, Marko. *Jürgen Moltmanns Theologie in Auseinedersetzung mit Ernst Bloch*. Frankfurt am Main, 1983; Pehar, Marija. *Schöpfung zwischen Trinität und Eschaton: Die Schöpfungslehre Jürgen Moltmanns im Gesamtkontext seiner Theologie*. Berlin, 2006; Škvorčević, Antun. *Ecclesiologia eshatologico-messianica di Jürgen Moltmann*. Rome, 1982.

7. Let us consider here Moltmann's claim, which, through Marx's theses on Feuerbach, best describes the intention of his early theology: "For the theologians the matter is not to provide a different interpretation of the world, the history and human being, but for *them* to be transformed in expectation of a divine transformation." Moltmann, *Theology of Hope*, 46.

interpretation of reality of the world and human being? This interest is at the heart of Moltmann's early theology, in particular in *Theology of Hope* and *The Crucified God*.

In this paper we will try to explore the theological assumptions of Moltmann's theology which, to borrow from Theodor W. Adorno, whose work *Negative Dialectics* Moltmann heavily relied on in his early works, allow us "not to philosophize about concrete things . . . but rather out of these things."[8]

This philosophy out of concrete things, or, rendered in perspective of Moltmann's thought, the theology emerging out of experiences and concrete events, without interpreting them on the basis of presupposed teachings and beliefs, but rather radically departing from them, builds a theology and a talk of God out of the concrete events and concrete experiences. The reason behind Moltmann's theology, as we strive to point out, does not derive solely from his well-known theological sources, such as Luther's and Hans-Joachim Iwand's theology of the cross, but also from the acceptance of Hegel's talk on the speculative Good Friday providing a framework for every thought on God, and the acceptance of the critical theory insights and negative dialectics of the members of the Frankfurt school, Adorno and Horkheimer in particular. Moltmann thus becomes a full-fledged representative of modern theology which has placed the area of possible experience and the revelation of God in history. Any talk of God can find its origin only in this history since God fully spoke only in history, and history is the stage of understanding of God. Or, in Moltmann's words, "The history of God is then to be thought of as the horizon of the world."[9]

---

8. Adorno, *Negative Dialectics*, 33.
9. Moltmann, *Crucified God*, 225.

WHERE IS GOD? THE ESSENTIAL IMPETUS OF MOLTMANN'S THEOLOGY

In his memoirs, Moltmann writes,

> During that night I cried out to God for the first time in my life and put my life in his hands. I was as if dead, and ever after received life every day as a new gift. My question was not, "Why does God allow this to happen?" but, "My God, where are you?" And there was the other question, the answer to which I am still looking for today: Why am I alive and not dead, too, like the friend at my side? I felt the guilt of survival and searched for the meaning of continued life. I knew that there had to be some reason why I was still alive. During the night I became a seeker after God.[10]

The event that Moltmann describes above is Operation Gomorrah (July 1943) in which the Allies bombed Hamburg, killing more than forty thousand civilians. Moltmann fought in this conflict as a young German artillerist, and a friend of his died that night by his side.

This question, a key question for Moltmann's entire early thought and a foundation for the overall theology of the crucified God, including its motifs, is also a key question for a theology that is now commonly called "theology after Auschwitz." Rather than delving deeply into the divine being, theologians after Auschwitz, with J. Moltmann and J. B. Metz being the most prominent ones in Germany, focused their theology on the historical and concrete place of God's revelation, i.e., the cross of Christ, to respond not only to the question "where is God?," but to the discussion on the meaning of evil and suffering, radically challenging the existence of a good and just God of traditional theology.[11] In the words of

---

10. Moltmann, *Broad Place*, 17.

11. So Wiesel: "Why, but why would I bless Him? Every fiber in me rebelled. Because He caused thousands of children to burn in His mass graves? Because He kept six crematoria working day and night, including Sabbath and the Holy Days? Because in His great might, He had created Auschwitz, Birkenau, Buna, and so many other factories of death? . . . I was the accuser, God the accused." Wiesel, *Night*, 67, 23.

Eberhard Jüngel, a younger contemporary of Moltmann and Metz, the modern age's question about God is not, "as opposed to classical metaphysical tradition, whether there is God or what is God, but where is God?"[12] Jüngel will base this on the well-known question, "Where has God disappeared?" that Nietzsche asked in his work *Gay Science,* representing, in Jüngel's opinion, "an expression of experience that God can no longer be grasped as a description of something that is entirely above, whereby preserving the focus of distinguishing between the Above and Below."[13]

In order to answer the question, "Where is God?" all three authors, in particular Moltmann, who is of our primary interest, places the question of God and his being within his revelation culminating at the end of the Jesus's historical process, namely, his crucifixion.

ATHEISM AS A CONTEXT FOR THE TALK OF GOD

Moltmann already took this path in elaborating his *Theology of Hope.* Aside from the future-oriented character of Christian theology, whereby "from first to last, and not merely in the epilogue, Christianity is eschatology, is hope, forward looking and forward moving, and therefore also revolutionizing and transforming the present,"[14] the foundations of Moltmann's early theology lie in his discovery of Hegel's speculative Good Friday. That discovery is revealed in "the pure concept or infinity as the abyss of nothingness in which all being is engulfed, must signify the infinite grief [of the finite] purely as a moment of the supreme Idea, and no more than a moment. Formerly, the infinite grief only existed historically in the formative process of culture. It existed as the feeling that 'God Himself is dead,' upon which the religion of more recent times rests . . . Thereby it must re-establish for philosophy that the absolute Passion, the speculative Good Friday in place of the historic

---

12. Jüngel, *God as the Mystery of the World,* 63.
13. Ibid., 64.
14. Moltmann, *Theology of Hope,* 2.

Good Friday. Good Friday must be speculatively re-established in the whole truth and harshness of its God-forsakenness."[15]

Moltmann does not expound on the idea of the death of God by finding its meaning within Hegel's philosophy, but takes it rather as a starting point to explain the modern experience of the world. Moreover, the idea of the death of God defining modern philosophy and experience must become a point of departure for talk about God in respect of theology as well, or as Moltmann claims, "Theology must accept the 'cross of the present' (Hegel), its godlessness and godforsakenness."[16] Namely, the place of theological discussion must take into account the situation of modern experience of *harsh words* about the death of God, and refrain from apologetically confirming the *spirit of resurrection* against this world, judging and shunning the godless world in its reasoning, but accept that this statement on the death of God lies at the heart of Christian theology and that this event of the death of God shall be the foundation for a whole new metaphysics and a Christian talk resting on the experience of the world awash with pain and hopelessness.

Taking situations of the death of God, or rather the atheistic situations of modern experience as a point of departure is the only appropriate talk of God, as Moltmann would put it.[17]

The key to Moltmann's theology and the possibility of its concretization seems to lie precisely in the acceptance of the atheistic situation of the modern age. With this goal in mind, Moltmann uses Luther's theology of the cross, allowing him to initiate the talk of God in its modern-day expression and stripped of traditional

---

15. Hegel, *Faith and Knowledge*, 190–91. On the analysis which Moltmann accepted in interpreting the speculative Good Friday as godforsakenness of the whole reality, see Marsch, *Gegenwart Christi in der Gesellschaft*, 241.

16. Moltmann, *Theology of Hope*, 46.

17. In his now famous conversation with Ernst Bloch relating to Bloch's motto "Only an atheist can be a good Christian" expressed at the beginning of Bloch's *Atheism in Christianity*, Moltmann proposed the following reversal of the phrase: "Only a Christian can be a good atheist," which Bloch finally accepted and placed at the beginning of the book. On this, see Moltmann, *History and the Triune God*, 145; and Bloch, *Atheism in Christianity*.

metaphysics and theology, which, as he states in the introduction to his *Crucified God*, grapples with the question of its identity and relevance.

> The Christian life of theologians, churches and human beings is faced more than ever today with a double crisis: the crisis of relevance and the crisis of identity . . . The more theology and the church attempt to become relevant to the problems of the present day, the more deeply they are drawn into the crisis of their own Christian identity.[18]

The crisis of identity of churches and theology itself, as Moltmann insistently points out, derives from their understanding not only of their essence but also of their mission.

In order to shape a theology incorporating in its core this modern-day problem of the death of God, Moltmann takes Hegel's speculative insight into the death of God, i.e., the speculative Good Friday. The speculative Good Friday is mentioned for the first time at the very end of Hegel's early philosophy, i.e., in his *Early Theological Writings*,[19] as Hermann Nohl, the first editor of Hegel's early writings, named them. Hegel used it in his three-pronged approach:

1. to counter Kant's philosophy—as the endless notion descending into the abyss of nothingness,

2. to counter the Lutheran orthodoxy of his time, in particular that of Tübingen where he studied from 1789 to 1793—as a feeling on which modern-day religion rests, and

3. to counter Schelling, his contemporary—the death of God as the moment of the highest idea.[20]

---

18. Moltmann, *Crucified God*, 1.
19. Hegel, *Theologische Jugendschriften*.
20. On Hegel's development from 1789–1802, see the most in-depth reports and analyses by Dieter Henrich in "Historische Voraussetzungen von Hegels System," 41–73, and elsewhere. On the beginnings of German idealism and its influence in shaping Hegel's thought, see Beiser, *German Idealism*, especially pp. 349–577.

The expression of the death of God was recognized as the theological idea *par excellence* by theologians, in particular those of the second half of the twentieth century. Although representing the core idea of Christian theology and faith, it gained its rightful place and significance only in the modern age and through Hegel himself:

> It was Georg Friedrich Wilhelm Hegel who introduced talk of the death of God into philosophy and in doing so was well aware that he was using a theological expression.[21]

His discussion on the speculative Good Friday, or death of God, had a profound impact on all of those theological and philosophical currents, especially on the so called "Young Hegelians" who found it the best way of describing the modern-day experience and, as Jüngel rather thoroughly elaborated in his classic work *God as the Mystery of the World*, the natural path of metaphysics culminating in the expression of the death of God, and receiving its final blow in Nietzsche's eponymous proclamation. Although the purpose of this text is not to dwell upon this process, we will consider how this theological explication of the understanding of the death of God—"the situation . . . interpreted by expounding the statement of Hegel and Nietzsche"[22]—determines to a large extent the possibility of Moltmann's talk about the cross, the death of God, as the very core of the overall Christian theology and talk of God.

Moltmann builds on the modern-day experience of the world, which in Hegel's theological exposition of the speculative Good Friday rests on the death of God as the event not only marking the core of Christian theology in the sense of Jesus's expiatory death on the cross, but also lying "at the foundations of modern experience of self and the world."[23] The exposition of Hegel's *speculative*

---

21. Jüngel, *God as the Mystery of the World*, 63.
22. Moltmann, *Theology of Hope*, 174.
23. Ibid.

Good Friday[24]—or, in Moltmann's words, the "epiphany of the eternal as subject"[25]—into *historical* Good Friday, Moltmann owes to Luther's insights as well as to observations from the members of the Frankfurt school, in particular those of Theodor Adorno. However, Moltmann will entirely preserve his position as a theologian whose core of the interpretation of reality and self-experience of the world will always remain the cross of Christ *challenging and interpreting everything*—an expression drawn from Luther, which lies at the heart of Luther's as well as Moltmann's theology of the cross. As opposed to Hegel, Moltmann historicizes the event of the death of God to underscore the uniqueness of the event of Christ's death on the cross:

> As I adopted Hegel's interpretation of "speculative Good Friday" in my book in order to make a universal meaning of historical Good Friday understandable, now I have to undertake a reverse research in order to integrate, radicalize, and establish the experiences and perspectives contained in the notion of "speculative Good Friday," within the Christ's "historical Good Friday" as the event that happened once for all. This is the opposite approach to that of Hegel's. If Good Friday, which "was otherwise only historic," is to be universalized into the night of godforsakenness and "the abyss of Nothing into which the whole being descends," we have to historicize in a Christian way that Good Friday, which is universal, in order to accept the memories of its overcoming.[26]

Such acceptance and foundation of theology will allow Moltmann to base the very core of Christian theology and the talk of God on concrete events and experiences, not only of the crucified one, but of every believer or religious institution that understands

---

24. This is how Hegel explains the need for speculative Good Friday in a correspondence: "In Swabia we say of something which happened long ago, 'It occurred so long since that it will soon no longer be true.' Christ likewise died for our sins so long ago that it will soon no longer be true." Hegel, *Jenaer Schriften*, 358, quoted in Küng, *Incarnation of God*, 174.

25. Moltmann, *Theology of Hope*, 151.

26. Moltmann, "Antwort auf die Kritik der *Theologie der Hoffnung*," 224.

this *word of the cross* as its standing challenge, the place of its mission, and the possibility of the talk of God in contemporary society. This reversal of the talk of God, as well as knowledge of God, from concrete towards universal, i.e., from a concrete event as the sole groundwork for a universal event, makes Moltmann not only a profound modern author, both in terms of philosophy and theology, but also an author who entirely *contextualizes* the talk of God, made possible only through concrete experiences and concrete identities.

By historicizing God, by understanding the world and its horizon as the only place of God's revelation, and the fullness of existence of believers and churches, guided by Jesus's historical process culminating on the cross, Moltmann builds his entire theology on a concrete event defining God's being and consequently the existence of believers and churches.

What are the reasons for Moltmann's epistemological turn and reversing of the interpretation of revelation? First, Luther's theology of the cross has to be acknowledged as the most important influence on Moltmann. As the two main items for his theology of the crucified one, Moltmann takes the nineteenth and twentieth theses from Luther's Heidelberg Disputation, held in 1518, that is, at the very beginning of the Reformation and "at the climax of his 'decision for reformation.'"[27]

> Thesis 19: He is not rightly called a theologian who perceives and understands God's invisible being through his works. That is clear from those who were such "theologians" and yet were called fools by the apostle in Romans 1.22. The invisible being of God is his power, Godhead, wisdom, righteousness, goodness, and so on. Knowledge of all these things does not make a man wise and worthy.[28]
>
> Thesis 20: But he is rightly called a theologian who understands that part of God's being which is visible and directed towards the world to be presented in suffering

27. Moltmann, *Crucified God*, 214.
28. Ibid.

and in the cross. That part of God's being which is visible and directed towards the world is opposed to what is invisible, his humanity, his weakness, his foolishness . . . So it is not enough and no use for anyone to know God in his glory and his majesty if at the same time he does not know him in the lowliness and shame of his cross . . . Thus true theology and true knowledge of God lie in Christ the crucified one.[29]

By accepting Luther's fundamental theses on the theology of the cross, Moltmann accepts its outcome, i.e., that true theology and true knowledge of God lie in the crucified one, but not its background and its causes. Following in Paul's footsteps, Luther introduces the theology of the cross as "foolishness" (1 Cor 1:18–25) in contrast to the theology relying on God's glory displayed in his majesty.

What in terms of theology of the cross were Greeks for Paul, and what humanistic man and "man's inhuman concern for self-deification through knowledge and works,"[30] was for Luther, becomes for Moltmann all such theology failing to adopt the cross as the center of its reflection, and thus failing to derive any sociopolitical and ontological consequences from it; in other words, all such theology interpreting the experience by using God as the objective and immutable givenness rather than shaping the talk of God out of that experience.

Consequently, as the core fact for any talk about God's being, Moltmann in his *Crucified God* introduces the historical process of Jesus Christ as a concrete historical event embodying the divineness of God and his nature. For Moltmann, the historical process

---

29. Ibid., 217.

30. Ibid., 68–69. With this Moltmann adopts Luther's theology of the cross as the criticism of humanism and humanistic man rather than the criticism of medieval scholastics. There are various viewpoints on the causes and background to Luther's theology of the cross, as evident in Lohse, *Martin Luther's Theology*, 36 ("The phrase *theologia crucis* does not challenge only scholastics but also Erasmus's humanism") as well as Loewenich, *Luther's Theology of the Cross*.

of Jesus Christ ending in the death on the cross includes three causes of death based on his historical existence:

1. Jesus's death as the death of a religious blasphemer.
2. Jesus's death as the death of a political rebel.
3. Jesus's death as the death of the godforsaken.[31]

Moltmann stresses the importance of these three reasons for Jesus's death on the cross not only to provide a mere depiction of the earthly life of Jesus of Nazareth or to elucidate another aspect or dimension of his historical existence, but also to bring to the fore some deeply theological considerations. By accepting that the historical existence of Jesus of Nazareth is the revelation of God himself,[32] the entire historical process of Jesus thus becomes the revelation of God himself. Only by exploring the historical Jesus and observing his context and causes of his death on the cross can we begin to talk about the nature of God himself.

Following his pre-established approach of placing the revelation of God on the cross,[33] as the culmination of Jesus's earthly life, we cannot but conclude that the revelation and nature of God may only be comprehended through Jesus's historical process. Moltmann consequently introduces a sociopolitical dimension into the existence of believers and churches as an inevitable consequence of the revelation of God in Christ, adopting Luther's fundamental stance "that God's revelation in Jesus Christ can in [no] way be

---

31. For an in-depth account on the causes of the death of Jesus, see *Crucified God*, 144–79, as well as a critical review of Moltmann's reasons for Jesus's death in Welker, *God the Revealed*, 172–79.

32. "Christian faith does not have a new idea of God, but rather finds itself in a different God-situation. It is defined through the passion of God and the cross of Christ." Moltmann, "The Crucified God and the Apathetic Man." Moltmann, *Crucified God*, 78.

33. On the difficulties of Luther's dual exposition of the theology of the cross representing, on the one hand, the *only* place of God's revelation and, on the other hand, stating that God in his glory and majesty can be *simultaneously* comprehended in humility and shame of the cross, as well as on the consequences of such twofold understanding in relation to the exposition of the theology of the cross in Hegel and Nietzsche, see Welker, *God the Revealed*, 141–42.

perceived or grasped through some 'absolute speculation' concerning God that ignores the humanity of Christ. God's revelation simply cannot be grasped through metaphysical speculation."[34]

The divinity of Christ to which Luther refers above, in Moltmann's view, represents Jesus's earthly path and all the causes leading him to the cross. Unlike Luther, who extended the theology of the cross from soteriological to epistemological theory, from the cross as a means and place of salvation to a new form of knowledge of God, Moltmann extends it onto the trinitarian and sociopolitical dimension that he reads from the cross.[35] Although the new epistemological dimension of God on the cross figures prominently in Moltmann's work, in which he contrasts the epistemological principle "like seeks after like" with the dialectical principle of "revelation in the opposite," the soteriological dimension of Christ's work hardly plays any role in Moltmann's opus. Traditional theologies that regard Jesus as a sacrifice, the one made for the sins of mankind and see Jesus's historical process from that perspective, in particular the death on the cross, are transformed by Moltmann into a theology where Jesus is also viewed as a victim of concrete historical, religious, and sociopolitical events and decisions of the time. By historicizing the causes of the death of God, or rather by reading the nature of divine being through the concrete history of Jesus of Nazareth, this *a priori* notion of God or the mapped-out course of the historical Jesus, utterly irrelevant for such theology since the act of salvation on the cross is the only one bearing any relevance, could almost be described along the lines of Hegel's well-known assertion that God before his incarnation could be regarded as a mere "abstract generality," and this also relates to the teaching on God that does not rely on concrete earthly revelation of God in Jesus.

As already pointed out, Moltmann will outline this path through three dimensions essential for establishing a new theology, including on the one hand a sociopolitical element, and

---

34. Welker, *God the Revealed*, 145.
35. On Moltmann's critique of Luther's theology of the cross, see Moltmann, *Crucified God*, 69–70.

on the other hand providing an answer to the key modern-age question *Where is God?* which gained urgency in catastrophes of the Second World War, in particular relating to Auschwitz.[36] Theological thought after Auschwitz, witnessing the disintegration of all dogmatic teachings on the good and almighty God, was brilliantly touched upon in the following words of Adorno: "No word intoned from on high, not even a theological one, exists rightfully after Auschwitz without a transformation."[37] This rightfulness of theological talk in Auschwitz is radically challenged not only on account of its generality, and the inability to correlate its fundamental tenets with the concrete reality directly hitting and destroying the notions of God which do not acknowledge that reality, but also on account of its failure to respond to the following fundamental question of the overall human expression relating to God: *Where is God in the midst of suffering of the innocent?*

The first three dimensions—the political, social, and religious ones—Moltmann finds in Jesus's death on the cross as a blasphemer and a rebel. The third dimension, of utmost interest here, on "the true inner pain of his suffering and death,"[38] Moltmann finds in the cry of Jesus on the cross *My God, why hast thou forsaken me?* He takes this cry from the passion narrative in the Gospel of Mark, the earliest one serving as the background for two other synoptic gospels. For Moltmann, the cry of Jesus is the core of his trinitarian reflection as well as the answer to the question on God that Jesus, as the one who lived and acted on behalf of that God, asks

---

36. Although, Moltmann will not call his theology "theology after Auschwitz," as identified by historians of theology of the second half of the twentieth century, but rather theology after the crucifixion of Jesus. However, the main context and the source of the overall theology emerging after the Second World War, in particular the one focusing on suffering and hopelessness (J. B. Metz, D. Sölle), is undoubtedly the Holocaust and the theological response to this "contingency shock." All these dimensions, not only primarily theological ones, are at the core of Moltmann's work providing it not only with theological vigor but also with the essential contextuality and concreteness of historical events.

37. Adorno, *Negative Dialectics*, 367.

38. Moltmann, *Crucified God*, 147.

emphatically. The cry on the cross is in fact the crux of Moltmann's theology.

The same question *My God, where are you?* that Moltmann asks at the beginning of his theological path is the one all theologies after the Holocaust are grappling with (in particular that of Elie Wiesel) namely *Where is God?* and *How did God let this happen?* With this cry Moltmann in fact wants to respond to the question asked, but also, in a completely radical way, interpret the scream and the cry of a concrete human being appealing to God. At one point in his book, illustrating the essential tone of Moltmann's theology, although Moltmann does not directly refer to it, Adorno writes: "Perennial suffering has as much right to expression as a tortured man has to scream."[39] Rather than only giving suffering the right to expression, or allowing those oppressed to express their experience, this right of suffering to expression primarily contains the very origin and the core of any talk, including the theological one. Since, according to Moltmann, the experience of suffering makes people ask profound questions on God, it is the source and birth place of theology.[40]

In this spirit, Moltmann gave right to the cry of the crucified one, thus allowing any talk of God to be shaped out of it, but this time significantly different from majority of Christian theology which is the subject of Moltmann's criticism.

METAPHYSICS OUT OF SUFFERING?

Taking suffering, specifically Christ's suffering on the cross as the basis for all theology, Moltmann outlined a theological program surpassing to a great extent the traditional talk of God allowing for a vast array of new possibilities of articulating the core of Christian

---

39. Adorno, *Negative Dialectics*, 362.

40. "A fundamental point of departure for the question about God and the understanding of Christ's passion is the experience of suffering." Moltmann, *The Future of Creation*, 67. Moltmann here directly relies on Dietrich Bonhoeffer who expressly stated in his letters from prison that only through suffering can we speak of God and God's being. Cf. Bonhoeffer, *Prisoner for God*, 164.

faith. Thus Moltmann will point out that "with the Christian message of the cross of Christ, something new and strange has entered the metaphysical world. For this faith must understand the deity of God from the event of the suffering and death of the Son of God and thus bring about a fundamental change in the orders of being of metaphysical thought and the value tables of religious feeling."[41]

Thinking God out of a concrete event for Moltmann means thinking God out of complete godforsakenness of Good Friday. Much in the vein of Hegel's speculative Good Friday, Moltmann interprets Good Friday as godforsakenness of the *entire* reality by God, rather than merely an event related to the person of Jesus Christ which ultimately bears a trinitarian importance for Moltmann.

> If this very atheism—as it has been most profoundly understood by Hegel and Nietzsche—derives from the nihilistic discovery made on the "speculative Good Friday," that "God is dead," then the only real way of vindicating theology in face of this reality . . . will be in terms of a theology of resurrection . . . Such a theology must accept the "cross of the present" (Hegel), *its godlessness and godforsakenness.*[42]

For such atheistic talk of God, stripped of any theistic explanation of reality, human being, and God, Moltmann draws on several sources defining in the main his overall theological discussion. First of them is of course Bonhoeffer with his well-known statement that "we have to live in the world *etsi Deus non daretur*,"[43] but also that fundamental Hegel's "feeling that 'God Himself is dead,' upon which the religion of more recent times rests."[44]

However, if we would embark on a quest to find the real source of Moltmann's atheism in relation to all theological expressions, then we would certainly find it in the death cry of Jesus *My God, why hast thou forsaken me?*, and all the consequences of this

41. Moltmann, *Crucified God*, 222.
42. Moltmann, *Theology of Hope*, 68 (my emphasis).
43. Bonhoeffer, *Prisoner for God*, 163.
44. Hegel, *Faith and Knowledge*, 190.

cry for ontology, and social and political theory. The cross as the only point of the talk of God thus becomes the point of destruction of any metaphysics that does not speak of God out of godforsakenness of Jesus on the cross, viewed, as we have seen, by Moltmann as the godforsakenness of the reality itself. All those images of God adorning the traditional metaphysical theologies and philosophies dissipate on the cross since "in the metaphysical concept of God from ancient cosmology and the modern psychological concept of God, the being of the Godhead, of the origin of all things or the unconditioned mover, as the zone of the impossibility of death, stands in juxtaposition to human being as the zone of the necessity of death."[45]

God who cannot suffer, Moltmann says, is not the God of Christian theology, understood as *theologia crucis* since the death *of God and in God* happened on the cross. The impossibility of God's suffering, his *apathy*, adorning all images of God as inherited from Greek or Aristotle's metaphysics, put the event of the cross into a broader narrative of Jesus's earthly path, his death and resurrection, without granting it a special place as demanded by all theologies which will, following Luther's reasoning, require the cross to be the measure of everything and the theology itself (*crux sola est nostra theologia*). Such theology sees in the cross nothing but the *superfluous* fact having hardly any bearing on the divine life or theological talk itself, except on those theologies and devotions centering on the cross as the object of their following, mysticism or compassion with the passion of Christ.[46]

Moltmann reverses this logic of the cross and puts the cross at the heart of his theology, in such a way that the cross no longer represents only a historical event which, as Hegel once put it, *happened so long ago that it will soon no longer be true*, but also an ever-present challenge in the life of churches, as well as an individual believer, and more importantly an event affecting God's being itself. For Moltmann, the cross is at the same time the end

---

45. Moltmann, *Crucified God*, 221.

46. A short overview and criticism of such theologies can be found in chapter 2 of *Crucified God*, pp. 50–73.

of all metaphysics because metaphysical theism is not applicable to it,[47] and the possibility of a new metaphysics with suffering (of God) as its foundation.

What does this suffering mean for the development of a new metaphysics and this-worldly and historical existence of human being, religious communities, and their institutions?

Placing the *locus* of historical revelation of God exclusively in the passion of Christ on the cross allows Moltmann to locate *the event* of God among those who, like Jesus, were and still are the victims of concrete religious, social, and political injustices. Presenting the cross as a consequence of Jesus's conflict with the religious, social, and political authorities of the time, in a theologically unforgettable way Moltmann situates the very revelation of God on the *margins* of those religious, social, and political areas, rather than in their center, which is a major shift in relation to both traditional theology and the modern criticism of religion:

> The modern criticism of religion can attack the whole world of religious Christianity, but not this unreligious cross. There is no pattern for religious projections in the cross. For he who was crucified represents the fundamental and total crucifixion of all religion: the deification of the human heart, the sacralization of certain localities in nature and certain sacred dates and times, the worship of those who hold political power, and their power politics.[48]

Does this understanding of the cross, as expounded by Moltmann above, represent a revolution not only in relation to the concept of God, but also in relation to the earthly activities of believers and their religious institutions?

Written in 1972, just a few years after the major student revolutions swept across Europe, *The Crucified God* abounds with critical showdowns with both the traditional theology and the modern-day churches, which have turned into fossils of dogmas and morals, while adapting to this world to such an extent that no

47. Ibid., 225.
48. Ibid., 33.

word of the cross, as the foundation of Christian theology, can free them from temptation to adjust their convictions and their core mission to the current sociopolitical interests. This revolutionary understanding of theology is mostly reflected in the dialogical counterparts Moltmann chose in his early phase to articulate his thought, primarily Ernst Bloch in *Theology of Hope* and later Theodor Adorno and Max Horkheimer in *The Crucified God*.

We may accuse Moltmann of one-sidedness, or for reading the entire event of God from the perspective of the cross,[49] but he could hardly be reproached for radical way in which he understands the cross and its consequences for the overall theology and the life of believers and religious institutions in modern societies, because the life of believers and churches in modern society is to a large degree marked by the tension surrounding their relevance for the problems of modern societies and man.

This relevance tension or the *identity-involvement dilemma*, as Moltmann would call it,[50] depends entirely on the understanding of the basic element of the overall Christian existence and faith, or rather on the understanding of the cross. Will the cross be the place of consolation and confirmation of our own Christian identity, as the cross most frequently represents it and not only in terms of popular devotion, but also in cultural, civilizational and religious sense, or will it be the place of the original theological self-emptying (kenosis) of own identity, of the self-externalization (*Entäußerung*) into something different and other, whereby the different and the other represent a complete rejection of all foundations of identity, and mental and spiritual projections of God and our own faith. This all determines whether a believer is the one who will eschew all conflicts of the present day for the sake of the cross or the one who will take the plunge with his mental projections on God and his own soul for the sake of changing the current

---

49. On this, see discussions in Welker, *Diskussion über Jürgen Moltmanns Buch "Der gekreuzigte Gott,"* in particular contributions by L. M. Lochmann, H. H. Miskotte, and D. Migliore, as well as Moltmann's response in "Antwort auf die kritik an 'Der gekreuzigte Gott.'"

50. Moltmann, *Crucified God*, 15.

oppressive and repressive sociopolitical relations dehumanizing human being. Moltmann insistently pleads for the latter option:

> Only by self-emptying in encounter with what is alien, unknown and different does man achieve selfhood. If Christians empty themselves in this way in a situation of political conflict, then in fact they abandon the traditions, institutions and opinions, accepted in faith, in which they previously found their identity.[51]

Does this view represent a mere theology of revolution entirely in line with the spirit of Moltmann's time? Or can that event of "self-externalization" as the permanent identity of every human being, and especially those who appeal to the cross of the crucified one in their faith, be time and again reapplied to every identity of believers and religious institutions? With this radical, political, social, and existential concept of Good Friday Moltmann supplements and surpasses Luther's theology of the cross as well as Hegel's speculative Good Friday, since this historicization of the event of Good Friday through Jesus's historical process, while showing a wealth of meanings of the cross, allows Moltmann to extend the cross beyond human interests for salvation (constituting the soteriological dimension of the cross), the interests which see in this cross consolation and escape from their inescapable sinful existential state, making it in the full sense of that word *scandalous and insane,* but this time not for *Greeks* and *Jews,* as the traditional understanding of the cross goes, following Paul's identical statement on the nature of the cross, but for Christian community itself and the believer. The cross in Moltmann's understanding stands beyond consolation and all objective givenness, and destroys them. However, it does not destroy them in order to underscore any impossibility of the talk of God, thus aligning itself with apophatic theology which lacks any appropriate words for the divine, but to point to the only actual divine reality which consists of relinquishing our own identity and directing our gaze towards that margin, or more radically said, towards that area where nobody, and the

---

51. Ibid., 10.

Christian community in particular, wants to build their identity, for God "was not crucified between two candles on an altar, but between two thieves in the place of the skull, where the outcasts belong, outside the gates of the city."[52]

THE OUTCAST NATURE OF REVELATION AND CONDITIONS OF THE POSSIBILITY OF ITS REALIZATION

The concreteness of the revelation of God at the site of the criminals which is the cross causes theological talk happening and deriving from everything that is unrighteous and unsolicited in the realm of religion, as well as society and politics, and from everything that violates all norms of exalted religiosity or images of God confirming such religiosity. The "marginal" character of revelation that does not rely on lifting the religious reality above the world of conflicts but lives daily in those conflicts, *building its identity through them*, seems to give the stamp of permanence to Moltmann's theology and his book *The Crucified God*.

Externalization of own identity into the area of nonidentity, into the abyss of nothingness in which all being sinks (Hegel), as religious consciousness would see it, is an essential prerequisite for any talk of "a new heaven and a new earth" (Rev 21:1) constituting the goal of the overall Jesus's talk of the Kingdom of God, since, as extensively elaborated by Moltmann in his *Theology of Hope*, this *novum* "is itself summoned and empowered to creative transformation of reality,"[53] and this transformation can only happen if we turn our gaze to the reality of the crucified one, and the reasons that led to his crucifixion. In concrete terms, the realization of the Christian message is only possible through criticism of the overall metaphysical and theistic conceptions of God and the church, which builds its identity on the image of God who ensures consolation and an escape from this conflict-laden world. Human

---

52. Ibid., 35.
53. Moltmann, *Theology of Hope*, 34.

and Christian expression is only possible through this source, i.e., "the word of the cross" so as to make the crucified one not the ideal projection of faith, the faith seeking confirmation in safety of its salvation or in *lifting up of the soul to God*, but to build its identity *through*, *amid* and *on* the conflicts of the present time. This makes the existence of Christian churches and the believer entirely dependent on a given reality, its conflicts, insecurities, and challenges in order to build the identity of its social and political environment within this *novum*, which does not translate into a mere return to the cozy past but into something new that cannot happen without the "externalization" into non-identity. This externalization requires a complete criticism and an overthrow of all possible and existing religious perceptions, national and religious identities, and the obsessive quest for God in that which is solid, permanent and safe.

Can we, or rather may we, then take Moltmann's shaping of theology out of concrete situations of human being, society, and church as merely one of the possible *theories on God* for us to explore while being safely sheltered by religious projections? Or is it possible to understand such theology as a lasting warning to all our national, religious, and personal identities confirming the talk of God void of any direct relation to the reality shaping it, while at the same time that reality of conflicts and destruction of all objective givenness is directly emerging from *the naked cross* of Jesus Christ who was crucified in the name of such talk of God?

—Translated by Dragana Divković

BIBLIOGRAPHY

Adorno, Theodor W. *Negative Dialectics*. Translated by A. B. Ashton. London: Routledge, 1973.

Beiser, Frederick. *German Idealism: Struggle against Subjectivism, 1781–1801*. Cambridge: Harvard University Press, 2008.

Bloch, Ernst. *Ateizam u kršćanstvu*. Translated by Hrvoje Šarinić. Zagreb: Naprijed, 1986.

Bonhoeffer, Dietrich. *Prisoner for God: Letters and Papers from Prison*. Edited by Eberhard Bethge. Translated by Reginald H. Fuller. New York: Macmillan, 1959.

Đogo, Darko. "Politikantska ili politička teologija 1945–2010 ili o (ne) mogućnosti jedne jugoslavenske političke teologije." In *Opasna sjećanja i pomirenje: kontekstualna promišljanja o religiji u postkonfliktnom društvu*, edited by Srđan Sremac et al., 93–129. Rijeka: Ex libris, 2011.

Hegel, G. W. F. *Faith and Knowledge*. Translated by W. Cerf and H. S. Harris. Albany, NY: State University of New York Press, 1977.

———. *Theologische Jugendschriften*. Translated by Hermann Nohl. Tübingen: J. C. B. Mohr, 1907.

Henrich, Dieter. "Historische Voraussetzungen von Hegels System." In *Hegel im Kontext*, 41–72. Frankfurt am Main: Suhrkamp, 1967.

Jüngel, Eberhard. *God as the Mystery of the World: On the Foundation of the Theology of the Crucified One in the Dispute between Theism and Atheism*. Translated by Darrell L. Guder. London: T. & T. Clark, 1983.

Küng, Hans. *The Incarnation of God*. Translated by J. R. Stephenson. Edinburgh: T. & T. Clark, 1987.

Loewenich, Walter von. *Luther's Theology of the Cross*. Translated by Herbert J. A. Bouman. Minneapolis: Augsburg, 1976.

Lohse, Bernhard. *Martin Luther's Theology: Its Historical and Systematic Development*. Translated and edited by Roy A. Harrisville. Minneapolis: Fortress, 1999.

Luther, Martin. "Heidelberška rasprava." In *Temeljni reformatorski spisi* 2. Translated by Goran Gajšak. Zagreb: Demetra, 2007.

Marsch, Wolf-Dieter. *Gegenwart Christi in der Gesellschaft: Eine Studie zu Hegels Dialektik*. Munich: Kaiser, 1965.

Moltmann, Jürgen. "Antwort auf die Kritik der Theologie der Hoffnung." In *Diskussion über die "Theologie der Hoffnung"*, edited by Wolf-Dieter Marsch, 201–38. Munich: Kaiser, 1967.

———. *A Broad Place: An Autobiography*. Translated by Margaret Kohl. London: SCM, 2007.

———. "The Crucified God and the Apathetic Man." In *The Experiment Hope*, edited and translated by M. Douglas Meeks, 69–84. 1975. Reprint. Eugene, OR: Wipf & Stock, 2003.

———. *The Crucified God: The Cross of Christ as Foundation and Criticism of Christian Theology*. Translated by R. A. Wilson and John Bowden. Minneapolis: Fortress, 1993.

———. *The Future of Creation: Collected Essays*. Translated by Margaret Kohl. Minneapolis: Fortress, 2007.

———. *History and the Triune God: Contributions to Trinitarian Theology*. Translated by John Bowden. New York: Crossroad, 1992.

———. *Raspeti Bog: Kristov križ kao temelj i kritika kršćanske teologije*. Translated by Željko Pavić. Rijeka: Ex libris, 2005.

———. "The Theology of the Cross Today." In *The Future of Creation: Collected Essays*, translated by Margaret Kohl, 59–79. Minneapolis: Fortress, 2007.

———. *Theology of Hope: On the Ground and the Implications of a Christian Eschatology*. Translated by James W. Leitch. Minneapolis: Fortress, 1993.

Šarčević, Ivan. "Kako preobraziti naš stari svijet." In *Javna vjera: kršćani i opće dobro*, by Miroslav Volf, 175–83. Translated by Zoran Grozdanov. Rijeka: Ex libris, 2013.

Welker, Michael., ed. *Diskussion über Jürgen Moltmanns Buch "Der gekreuzigte Gott."* Munich: Kaiser, 1979.

———. *Offenbarung Gottes: Christologie*. Neukirchen-Vluyn: Neukirchener, 2012.

Wiesel, Elie. *Night*. Translated by Marion Wiesel. New York: Hill and Wang, 2006.

3

The Development of Democratic Political Culture

Religions as Agents of Political Liberation? (Contextual Discussion Drawing on *The Crucified God*, by J. Moltmann)

—Alen Kristić

> *The cross of Jesus marks a divide between the human God who is freedom and love and the "counter-God" who keeps men under his sway and dominated by fear, like demons, and sucks them up into nothingness. However, "the crucified God" here cannot be interchanged with the "God of Christians," for by the terms of a psychological or sociological analysis the God of the Christians is not always the "crucified God." Only rarely is this the case. Even for historical Christianity the cross, if it is understood radically and down to its final consequences, is a scandal and foolishness.*[1]

---

1. Moltmann, *Crucified God*, 201.

Theology—Descent into the Vicious Circles of Death

INTRODUCTION

The Crucified God: The Cross of Christ as the Foundation and Criticism of Christian Theology, the monumental theological piece written by Jürgen Moltmann and published in 1972, culminates in the final chapter, whose title "Ways towards the Political Liberation of Man"[2] was once, and still is, considered highly provocative in today's postmodern circumstances marked by the quest for new forms of practicing the politics of emancipation.

Emboldened by a three-hundred-page theological discussion in the previous chapters, and building upon the psychological hermeneutics of liberation expounded in the penultimate chapter, titled "Ways towards the Psychological Liberation of Man,"[3] in the final chapter Moltmann boldly comes to grips with the invariably risky but inevitable account of the economic, social, and political consequences of the gospel:

> What is meant by the contemporization of the crucified God in the political religions of society? In what dimensions must a human society develop in the free sphere of the history of this God? What are the economic, social and political consequences of the gospel of the Son of Man who was crucified as a "rebel"?[4]

Within this framework and inspired in the first instance by the unflinching conviction that the "freedom of faith is lived out in political freedom"[5] and that "the freedom of faith therefore urges men on towards liberating actions"[6]—this insight in particular could be rightly considered to represent the central result of "pathetic theology," which Moltmann critically developed in *The Crucified God*, while bidding farewell to *apathetic theology* (Hellenism) which gave rise to "a metaphysical misunderstanding of the

---

2. See ibid., 331–56.
3. See ibid., 304–30.
4. Ibid., 331.
5. Ibid.
6. Ibid.

original meaning of the New Testament message,"[7] and specifically to the disfiguring and turning of Christianity into a violent ideology sacralizing secular political power whose violence is deeply rooted in the fear of historicity and mortality of all that is human—Moltmann resolutely states:

> The situation of the crucified God makes it clear that human situations where there is no freedom are vicious circles which must be broken through because they can be broken through in him. Those who take the way from freedom of faith to liberating action automatically find themselves cooperating with other freedom movements in God's history. Political hermeneutics calls especially for dialogue with socialist, democratic, humanistic and anti-racist movements.[8]

Now, in the case of political hermeneutics of faith from the perspective of the crucified God, Moltmann critically abandons the indifferent God of the Western metaphysics or ontotheology. However, the issue at hand here is not the politicization of the church. This critique is incessantly and quite presumptuously refuted by those expressing concern for orthodoxy, which in that case is nothing but the mask of one's own servitude to an apathetic God.[9] The heart of the matter here is in fact a critique of the oppressive theological church politics imbued with blasphemous indifference towards human vulnerability and misery, or more specifically:

> Political hermeneutics sets out to recognize the social and economic influences on theological institutions and languages, in order to bring their liberating content into the political dimension and to make them relevant towards really freeing men from their misery in certain vicious circles. Political hermeneutics asks not only what sense it makes to talk to God, but also what the function

---

7. Vattimo, *Jenseits des Christentums*, 179.
8. Moltmann, *Crucified God*, 332.
9. For more on this, see a very instructive discussion by Pavić, "Crux probat omnia!," 281–326.

of such talk is and what effect it has. Even here, none of the so-called substance of faith is lost; rather, faith gains substance in its political incarnations and overcomes its un-Christian abstraction, which keeps it far from the present situation of the crucified God. Christian theology must be politically clear whether it is disseminating faith or superstition.[10]

In other words, only by tearing off the shackles of metaphysical violence and abstract indifference from theological discourse—and this is exactly what Moltmann endeavors in *The Crucified God*—can the subversive memory of "political crucifixion and divine resurrection of Christ who was executed as a 'rebel'"[11] be restored back to the core of the church.

This departure allows for crucial realization that the church can in an authentic manner, not be, but time and again happen exclusively in the solidary and kenotic descent into the present situations of the crucified God.

What we are talking about here is putting into practice—or into the contemporary "circles of death" as Moltmann articulates it more closely—the program mapped out in *Gaudium et spes* containing the fundamental theology of the Second Vatican Council:

> The memory of the passion and resurrection of Christ is at the same time both dangerous and liberating. It endangers a church which is adapted to the religious politics of its time and brings it into fellowship with the sufferers of its time. It frees the church from politico-religious church politics for a critical Christian political theology. The new political theology is not concerned with the dissolution of the church into left-wing or right-wing politics, but with the Christianization of its political situation and function in terms of the freedom of Christ.[12]

The kenotic and solidary descent of the church into the contemporary situations of the crucified God, as the only authentic

10. Moltmann, *Crucified God*, 332.
11. Ibid., 341.
12. Ibid.

way of its own implementation, or implementation of the task it has been entrusted with—and this is what Moltmann comes to in *The Crucified God* after the Christian message has been finally stripped of the metaphysical patina—directly relates to the new understanding of political and state authority which, according to Moltmann, brings about the key obligation of a new critical political theology, that is, concrete perseverance in taking a clearly defined and mapped-out course of "desacralization, relativization and democratization."[13]

> If the Christ of God was executed in the name of the politico-religious authorities of his time, then for the believer the higher justification of these and similar authorities is removed. In that case political rule can only be justified "from below." Wherever Christianity extends, the idea of the state changes. Political rule is no longer accepted as God-given, but is understood as a task the fulfilment of which must be constantly justified. The theory of the state is no longer assertive thought, but justifying and critical thought . . . A critical political theology today must take this course of desacralization, relativization and democratization. If the churches become "institutions for the free criticism of society," they must necessarily overcome not only private idolatry but also political idolatry and extend human freedom in the situation of the crucified God not only in the overcoming of systems of psychological apathy, but also in the overcoming of the mystique of political and religious systems of rule which make men apathetic.[14]

It is exactly this point that this discussion will build on—most assuredly drawing on the insights and visions of *The Crucified God*—in its presentation and subsequent elaboration of a thesis on potential contribution of religions in the political liberation of human being in Bosnia and Herzegovina within a nearly forgotten and complex sphere of the development of democratic political culture, which is according to Moltmann, as already pointed out,

13. Ibid., 343.
14. Ibid., 342–43.

a crucial task of the new critical political theology: democratization which inevitably involves relativization and desacralization (of politics).

Undoubtedly, this will be a step-by-step approach with full appreciation for the fact that the failings of religion in Bosnia and Herzegovina (but also generally in the region) are primarily situated in the political sphere or, if you will, in the field of mutual permeation and entwining of religion and politics, whereby religion is (and has been) always focused on sacralizing and absolutizing politics, or adamantly opposed to everything with even a slight touch of democracy.[15]

At the very outset of this discussion, we will explore how transformation of the political system in Bosnia and Herzegovina (and generally in the region) in the 1990s failed to wipe out the centuries-long models of nondemocratic political culture and their adverse effects on the democratic functioning of the political system. This will lead us to conclude that the democratic consolidation of society in Bosnia and Herzegovina unconditionally requires investing systemic efforts in the development of democratic political culture. Moreover, we will take this argument further by claiming that this process will largely depend on whether religious communities in Bosnia and Herzegovina will keep insisting on the nondemocratic principles or finally turn to the democratic political socialization, or whether they would remain the agents of political servitude or turn into the agents of political liberation of man.

The second part of the discussion addresses a unique socio-infrastructural network of local religious communities that the overall religious communities in Bosnia and Herzegovina have at their disposal in terms of political socialization. After we point out that the shift of religious communities towards political socialization of the democratic political culture would not indicate a mere socially preferred adjustment but also a true religious catharsis, we will focus on exploring the predominant patterns of political socialization in local religious communities to see if considerations

---

15. See Kristić, *Religija i moć*, 1–330; and Kristić, *Tiranija religijskog*, 1–304.

on the interdependence between the development of the subjectivity of believers, who are rooted in local religious communities, in terms of their values and viewpoints, and the development of their civil and political subjectivity could be initiated in Bosnia and Herzegovina as well.

With this descent into the *base*, in a particular way we seem to stay true to Moltmann's "theological project," the underlying feature of which—and I dare say the key source of its enduring power to creatively inspire others until the present day—is to think out of the concrete things and for the concrete things, i.e., without fleeing into the abstractness, but above all without fleeing from human vulnerability and finality made disturbingly evident on the faces of our neighbors, our own faces, and our inner selves. To sum up, the price of good theology is an inexorable exposure to concrete situations or, as Moltmann would put it, a bold acceptance of the cross of reality.

The third part attempts to address the issue of a key precondition for religious communities in Bosnia and Herzegovina to live, or rather revive their own potential for socialization of the democratic political culture and thus provide—beyond the bounds of politicization of religion and nationalistically tainted religionization of politics—a concrete contribution to political liberation of man as outlined by Moltmann at the end of *The Crucified God*.

Nevertheless, our finding concerning this matter will not be any different from the one Moltmann came to in *The Crucified God*. The only effective way to overcome the fundamental source of the crisis of relevance in Christian life and the crisis of identity for Christian faith, which is closely related to it, is to part ways with "metaphysical mentality" (G. Vattimo). The key is to finally accept, and execute anti-metaphysical, or rather unreligious fate of Christian faith, as D. Bonhoeffer and G. Vattimo, though with substantial but in no way unbridgeable differences, would both put it.

The discussion, in terms of its essence and culmination, ends with a consideration and subsequent rough elaboration of what the concrete or contextual execution of the fundamental program of *The Crucified God* would involve for religions of Bosnia and

Herzegovina (and the whole region of Western Balkans), and predictably enough, this primarily includes kenotic and solidary descent of religions into the present situations of the crucified God or the present vicious circles of death. In our humble judgment, preliminary finding would indicate a much needed shift away from utopias of nationalistically religious ghettos towards heterotopias of the postwar transitional traumas. But before we embark on the implementation of the targeted program, let us briefly explore the mutually connected and interpenetrated vicious circles of death,[16] and their matching, mutually connected, and interpenetrated "ways towards liberation"[17] that Moltmann articulates in the final pages of *The Crucified God*, all the more so as they represent the program framework for our discussion.

For the vicious circle of poverty, situated in the economic dimension of life, liberation means the satisfaction of the material needs of human beings in terms of health, food, clothing and shelter. For the vicious circle of violence, situated in the political dimension of life, liberation means democracy, greater respect for human dignity, and taking political responsibility. For the vicious circle of racial and cultural alienation situated in the cultural dimension of life, liberation means establishing identity by recognizing others. For the vicious circle of the industrial pollution of nature, situated in the sphere of the relationship of society to nature, liberation means peace with nature. All in all, for the vicious circle of senselessness and godforsakenness, situated in the sphere of questions on the meaning of life, liberation means meaningful life and a life with fullness of meaning. Showing that "in the vicious circle of poverty, liberation must be called social justice; in the vicious circle of force, it must be called democratic human rights; in the vicious circle of alienation, it must be called identity in recognition; in the vicious circle of ecology, it must be called peace with nature; and in the vicious circle of meaninglessness, it must be called courage to be, and faith."[18] In fact, Molt-

---

16. Cf. Moltmann, *Crucified God*, 343–46.
17. Cf. ibid., 346–49.
18. Ibid., 351.

mann reminds us of the symbolic and sacramental constitution of Christianity—or more radically said, of its incarnational and kenotic structure—which in turn means that there can be no authentic Christian discourse on God without the concrete actions of liberation from the historically conditioned vicious circles of death—right here, right now.

Within this framework and going far beyond the idolatry of ideological fixation and its counterpart, i.e., idolatry of the normative force of the factualness, the concrete actions of liberation from the present vicious circles of death, according to Moltmann, thus become "real ciphers and material anticipations of the physical presence of God"[19] or "incarnations which point beyond themselves"[20] overcoming not only the temptation to reduce (Christian) salvation to the otherworldliness and abstractness but also to the present and factualness:

> In the vicious circle of poverty it can be said: "God is not dead. He is bread." God is present as bread in that he is the unconditional which draws near, in the present sense. In the vicious circle of force God's presence is experienced as liberation for human dignity and responsibility. In the vicious circle of alienation his presence is perceived in the experience of human identity and recognition. In the vicious circle of the destruction of nature God is present in joy in existence and in peace between man and nature. In the vicious circle of meaninglessness and god-forsakenness, finally, he comes forward in the figure of the crucified Christ, who communicates courage to be.[21]

We will end these introductory thoughts with Moltmann's words emphasizing once again the form and nature of the political responsibility of Christians who see the cross of Christ as the foundation and criticism of Christian theology, or rather Christian existence in general, with the urgent (though not only interreligious) and challenging question on the elements in other religious

19. Ibid., 352.
20. Ibid.
21. Ibid.

traditions (re)unveiling the *weak* points of God which the cross of Christ sheds light on, or in other words, the elements in other religious traditions exposing an indifferent God in the shape of an idolatrous freak behind which the religious and political power elites hide their insatiable will to power:

> Christianity did not arise as a national or a class religion. As a dominant religion of rulers it must deny its origin in the crucified Christ and lose its identity. The crucified God is in fact a stateless and classless God. But that does not mean that he is an unpolitical God. He is the God of the poor, the oppressed and the humiliated. The rule of the Christ who was crucified for political reasons can only be extended through liberation from forms of rule which make men servile and apathetic and the political religions which give them stability. According to Paul, the perfection of his kingdom of freedom is to bring about the annihilation of all rule, authority and power, which are still unavoidable here, and at the same time to achieve the overcoming of equivalent apathy and alienation. Christians will seek to anticipate the future of Christ according to the measure of the possibilities available to them, by breaking down lordship and building up the political liveliness of each individual.[22]

I. THE BURDEN OF NONDEMOCRATIC POLITICAL CULTURE

Unstable societies including those of former socialist states of Central and Southeastern Europe are strongly affected by the discussion on political structures and processes. However, their democratic consolidation will be a predetermined failure or turn into an interminably unfinished process if the widespread current tendencies of discrediting the issues of culture are not offset and reversed. Naturally, in this neglected set of issues, of particular import is the political culture, understood here as the overall

22. Ibid., 343.

temporally changeable set of beliefs, values, knowledge, feelings and attitudes of members of a society against political objects, processes and goals generated through interactions of historical traditions, structures of political institutions and principles of functioning of a political system. In concrete terms, it is about a pressing task of developing a civil and democratic political culture, which is inconceivable without a fully developed civil society.[23]

The Urgency of a New Political Culture

In addition to the Western theory of civil society, the project World Ethos (H. Küng),[24] and the dialogue between philosophy and theology (for instance, between J. Habermas and J. Ratzinger),[25] as a theoretical confirmation of the urgency to build a democratic political culture within the framework of democratic consolidation of unstable societies, politological consensus on a democratic political culture is seen as an extremely important factor for sustainability and rejuvenation of democracy. Understood as a dynamic process rather than a fixed condition, democracy is a result of the complex interrelationship between political culture and political structure.[26]

Rather than all the theoretical considerations and discussions, a closer examination into the fate of socialist countries of the Central and Southeastern Europe, including the countries of our region after the fall of communism will give us a far better indication that any democratic consolidation of unstable societies will be an exercise in futility without a developed democratic political culture in place.

Consequently, what we have here is a chasm between a new democratic institutional setup and the inherited political culture set against the basic democratic values—political tolerance,

23. Cf. Vujčić, *Politička kultura demokracije*, 1–396.
24. Cf. Küng, *Svjetski ethos za svjetsku politiku*, 1–317.
25. Cf. Habermas and Ratzinger, "Dijalektika sekularizacije," 185–208.
26. Cf. Vujčić, "Politička kultura i politička struktura (I)," 113–39; and Vujčić, "Politička kultura i politička struktura (II)," 144–57.

freedom, democratic norms such as equality before the law, human rights, right to difference, freedom of the press, and free elections (J. Gibson)—which is a major discrepancy affecting transitional societies. A specific aspect of this is "social dissonance"[27] of the religious communities in transitional societies. The sheer inconsistency between their verbal commitments to democracy in society and their own institutional life replete with nondemocratic practices is a clear indication of their failure to apply the teachings, primarily social teachings, to their own organization. It is the source of a pernicious process of their idolization and bias, ranging from opportunism to alliance, in relation to authoritarian regimes. It's an unequivocal illustration that the change of political system did not automatically annihilate the inherited models of political culture and their negative effects on democratic functioning of the political system. For this reason, the institutional constitution of democracy must be unconditionally followed by a long-term development of political culture; in other words, the matter at hand is the democratic (re)socialization and (re)education of society, whereby civil society plays a vital role.[28]

Rather than an innate quality acquired by birth, the development of democratic behavior and mindset follows a gradual process, just as every political culture is an artificial rather than a natural social phenomenon that takes a lot of time to develop but also to disappear, or as R.G. Dahrendorf shrewdly warned after the fall of the Berlin Wall by saying that it takes only 6 months to change a political system, 6 years to change an economy but 60 years to develop a civil society or a democratic political culture.

In particular, this statement voicing the urgency for transformation of nondemocratic mentalities and structures applies to religious communities in transitional societies.[29] It is exactly, though not exclusively, within this framework that the current crisis in Bosnia and Herzegovina should be examined, including

27. Volf, *Trinität und Gemeinschaft*, 17.

28. Cf. Vujadinović, "Civilno društvo i politička kultura," 21–33.

29. Cf. Marasović, "Demokratska očekivanja od Crkve u Hrvatskoj između minimalizma i maksimalizma," 23–70.

the inability and unwillingness of political figures to overcome it by exercising pragmatism and rational behavior—a key feature of contemporary politics.

Prisoners of a Nondemocratic Political Culture

Despite an apparent lack of any substantial empirical and theoretical enquiries into it, the political culture in Bosnia and Herzegovina appears to be incontrovertibly opposed to the democratic values and political culture rooted in those values. But the culprit is not to be found only in the current political crisis, a vestige of the *unfinished war*, or in the recent experience of socialism, but in the overall historical legacy of Bosnia and Herzegovina. Despite all the differentiations, its historical legacy in all its aspects has always been not only disinclined but adamantly opposed to democracy; in terms of politics, it has always been *authoritative*, in terms of culture *traditionalist*, in terms of society always *underdeveloped*, and in terms of values always *collectivistic* and *conservative*.

In the light of various contemporary types of political culture,[30] the predominant one in Bosnia and Herzegovina may be described as *parochial-subject* (G. Almond/S. Verba), *traditionalist* (D. J. Elazar), *hierarchical fatalist* (A. Wildavsky) or *conservative* (G. G. Brenkert).

Given a vast number of volumes written about this complex relationship between religion and politics ever since the fall of communism in the region, in particular along the lines of *politicization of religion and religionization of politics* and *religious nationalism*, the role of religious communities in terms of regional reception and models of political governance has hardly been touched upon.[31] We can add to this a pervasive disregard for the fact that religious communities in our region have always played and still play one of the key roles in the process of political socialization of

---

30. Cf. Vujčić, "Tipologija političke kulture," 98–131.

31. Cf. Šimac, "Kršćanin u politici i suvremenoj Europi," 541–61; and Dugalić, "Politička traganja Crkve u Hrvatskoj (1989–2007)," 483–539.

a nondemocratic political culture, as expected given our counter-democratic historical legacy.

Strongholds of Nondemocratic Political Culture

In addition to using their nondemocratic organization of powerful symbolic authority and thus rooted nondemocratic institutional life for bolstering nondemocratic aspirations in society[32] within the complex process of political socialization of nondemocratic political culture, religious communities have always primarily resorted to a unique social and infrastructural network of local religious communities (hereafter cited as LRC): Christian parishes and Islamic jamaats.

It is precisely on account of the penetrating political power of that network that the state and political party leaders have always unrelentingly striven to bring religious institutions, as the unrivaled champions of sociopolitical integration, under their sway luring them by earthly privileges:

> Namely, certain political structures of the countries in transition offered state aid to the church for certain areas of pastoral care, giving the impression that they are ready to help the church restore the same social privileges that it enjoyed before the Second World War. But in return they required church to conform to the system and waive any right to social critique.[33]

In other words, an obedient and conformist believer equals an obedient and conformist subject of the state, or rather an obedient and conformist follower of a nation or a political party. LRCs are, so to speak, the privileged places of their upbringing.

Rather than seizing upon a unique historical chance after the fall of communism and transforming into one of the key levers of political socialization of the democratic political culture, regional religious communities uncritically surrendered themselves to

---

32. Cf. Baum, "Crkva—za i protiv demokracije," 17–27.
33. Máté-Tóth and Mikluščák, *Nicht wie Milch und Hönig*, 52.

autocratic and authoritarian coryphei of national liberation, convinced that the national restoration would translate into religious one. As a rule, we are talking about *political converts* whose autocratism and authoritarianism, for all their democratic appearances, expose their deep-rootedness in the nondemocratic past of the region in the form of Bolshevized communism, which is why, largely through their efforts, the mentality of *dead communism* endured precisely in religious communities.

Certainly, this shift would not only include a mere adjustment of religious communities to the needs of society but also their true religious catharsis. This is to say that the authentic religious and socially acceptable mentality go hand in hand in this case: believers aware of themselves and their responsibility will also be concerned and responsible citizens, pillars of democratic society, i.e., the citizens aware of themselves and their responsibilities, and open for independent and solidary activities, concerned and responsible members of a religious community.

The fact that religious communities in our region still widely figure as the strongholds of nondemocratic political culture is all the more tragic given their unmatched potential to uphold a systematic development of the democratic political culture through their unique socio-infrastructural network of LRCs. Provided that they open up to the divine power, this could be a privileged place of expiation for all their historical faults, for "the danger is extreme, yet where the danger is, also grows the saving power."[34]

Surely, there are two preconditions for this to happen. *Ad extra*—a sound separation of religious communities from the state, political, and party structures of power, and a shift towards active cooperation with the structures of civil society:

> Any alliance between the state and the church shall be entirely severed. This will liberate the church from currying favor with the state, and the state will be liberated from incompetent meddling of the church in the state matters.[35]

---

34. Hölderlin, *Gedichte*, 348.
35. Mardešić, *Vjernici o ratu i miru*, 31.

Ad intra—democratization of institutional life of religious communities, in particular at the local level:

> It must be acknowledged that church life requires a certain amount of "democratization." If this word is not suitable and there are doubts about the symbol of "people of God," it is possible to replace it with other words such as "community" or "synodality."[36]

A clearer indication of what the shift of religious communities towards the political socialization of the democratic political culture might mean in concrete terms is provided by an exploration of the concrete forms of political socialization of the nondemocratic political culture in LRCs.

II. SOCIALIZATION OF NONDEMOCRATIC POLITICAL CULTURE

The criteria for the selection of multiple mechanisms of nondemocratic political socialization in LRCs shall be the fundamental democratic values, all the more so since they are to a large extent—and in the case of Catholic Church, social teachings rest entirely on the principles of personality, solidarity, subsidiarity, the common good, participation, and ability—advocated in social teachings of the religious communities. But what should be kept in mind—notably when "allocating" the responsibilities between religious heads, LRC leaders (imams and pastors), and worshippers—is that LRCs with regard to mentality and structure generally mirror the religious communities in terms of absolutist leadership and pyramidal arrangement.[37]

The Mechanisms of Nondemocratic Political Socialization

The scope of this discussion does not permit vital differentiation either between different religious communities—in fact, their

---

36. Queiruga, *La Chiesa oltre la democrazia*, 54.
37. See Kristić, "Vjerske institucije u BiH," 167–201.

LRCs and their leaders enjoy a different theological and organizational status—or different LRCs, depending on their regional (their belonging either to a religious and ethnic minority or majority) or urban/rural position, bearing in mind the predominantly rural background of LRC leaders which plays a crucial part in this process. With full awareness of widely different practices, this part will primarily focus on the predominant ones in Bosnia and Herzegovina when it comes to political socialization within the LRCs, in an effort to spark critical examination of the interdependence of the ways believers are nurtured and developed in LRCs and the development of their civic and political subjectivity in terms of their values and viewpoints. In fact, this discussion itself suggests an urgent need for empirical investigation of life in LRCs, primarily from the perspective of political socialization in order to elicit subsequent responses from sociology, political science, and (pastoral) theology; of course all this with a view to developing better practices. Although the predominant practices are formidable, there are still LRC leaders open for democratic and political socialization. Moreover, it is worth noting that, more often than not, they are the leaders of the war-ravaged and transition-impoverished LRCs.

Political Subjectivity

The monocratic exercise of authority, deeply engrained in LRCs even when there are pastoral, social or economic councils in place, reduces believers to passivized objects. Believers with benumbed subjectivity thus become citizens without political competence or any awareness of the potential for personal influence on politics.

Furthermore, the impossibility of participating in the selection of LRC leaders breeds distrust among believers when it comes to civic duty of political participation.

But when they stride into the *political square*, it is exactly this centralistic leadership of LRCs which drives their propensity to select autocratic and centralistic political figures and parties.

This exposure to tutoring in LRCs, not only in matters of faith but also, quite often, in matters of culture and politics, transforms believers into citizens susceptible to tolerating sacralization of politics, i.e., religious communities openly endorsing certain political figures or parties.

Taken all together—monocratic exercise of authority in LRCs, nonparticipation of believers in the selection of LRC leaders, and tutoring in matters of politics in LRCs—believers are drilled for immature LRC membership, immersing themselves in the community and losing personal responsibility. This serves as a strong footing for them to live out all other identities, in particular national and political identities and party affiliations, without a critical and freedom-enabling distance.

In short: *The suppression of believers' subjectivity paves the way for the suppression of political subjectivity and vice versa!*

Freedom

Alienation of believers from LRCs as their personal responsibility stands in stark contrast to the ostentatious identification of leaders with their LRCs, often even with the church or God himself. Armed with the shield of impunity *from below*, every criticism *from within* is dismissed as an attempt at destroying unity, and every criticism *from the outside* is declared a phobia. LRCs become closed to the *communication without dominance*. Unreserved obedience to LRC leaders is masked as congregational virtuousness. When believers are stripped of their freedom, in particular freedom of opinion and expression, in this way in their LRCs, they are also one step away from becoming citizens succumbing to the sway of political heads who take a self-defensive stand hiding behind *vital ethnic interest* (even the ethnicity itself), and the self-vindicating religious heads hiding behind the religious institutions (even God himself).

Indeed, the key players in this process are the media in LRCs, predominantly outlets of monologues and directives rather than the free exchange of opinions. This process lays the groundwork for "partitocratic media manipulation"[38] of believers in the social and political sphere, i.e., opportunistic and servile media at the service of political and economic, but also religious, centers of power.

In short: *The suppression of believers' freedom paves the way for the suppression of civil liberties, and vice versa!*

Pluralism

Although strongly advocating faith as a personal choice, pluralism is incessantly demonized in LRCs. Every difference is met with hostility. As if something else, save the lack of faith, could jeopardize faith.

Brimming with enemies, the world is dualistically divided into the unconditionally good (*us*) and the unconditionally evil (*them*). Fear of the other distorts LRC into a closed and constantly besieged fortification. Instead of freedom, openness, and hope, the existence of believers is defined by oppression, narrow-mindedness, and pessimism. The atmosphere of oppression even coming from the LRC itself excludes all those daring to think differently, regardless of whether in terms of religion or politics. There is no place for tensions of plurality as the source of vitality.

With the fear of pluralism instilled in them, believers start yearning for security which in the social and political sphere comes forth in the shape of nostalgia for a totalitarian and unitary, and preferably religion-based, social system. By demonizing the *left* and sacralizing the *right*, believers in LRCs are surrendered to the right-wing conservative political parties in the political and social sphere.

Rather than a personal choice reinvigorated time and again before a multitude of life's challenges, faith in LRCs is presented as a biological and static legacy, to be defended rather than creatively developed. Instead of renewed personal and rational assessment of political programs and achievements, the political affiliation of

---

38. Bojić, "Večernji H–B list," 4.

believers rests on deeply ingrained "political idolatrousness,"[39] a sort of political fanaticism relying on the conviction that the absolute good is embodied in a given sociopolitical system.

Once people grow accustomed to perceiving unity as conformism in LRCs, this perception is mirrored in the sociopolitical sphere as well, paving the way for portentous monopolizing of national and political sphere by a single political party. The same pattern of dualism and ghettoization followed in religious sphere is replicated in the sociopolitical sphere. Rather than a positive challenge to their growth in faith and humaneness, atheists or members of other faiths are seen as a threat to own identity. Likewise, people espousing different political causes or world views are hardly seen as partners but enemies, or indeed the absolute evil.

In short: *The suppression of religious pluralism paves the way for the suppression of pluralism in the sociopolitical sphere and vice versa!*

The Culture of Remembrance

LRCs are the arenas of resistance to pluralism, even when it comes to resisting dialogical pluralization of perspectives on the past. A monopoly on the historical truth, up until recently possessed by the communist regime, is ardently sought after. But without an open and honest dialogue on the past, through forgiveness and reconciliation, no rehabilitation of the transitional societies will be achieved.

The pulpits in LRCs resound with invocations of one's own national and religious sufferings and victims. They are the subject of prayer ceremonies and monuments as public *places of remembrance*, often erected even for executioners of the victims belonging to other religious and national communities, for the pitiful purpose of achieving one's own religious and national purity, now quite often even territorially guaranteed.

---

39. Cf. Frank, "Rušenje idola," 771–828.

"Sensitivity to the suffering of others"[40] as the foundation of monotheistic ethos, but also "the need to lend a voice to suffering [as] a condition for all truth,"[41] or a condition for the truthfulness of memories, has long been banished from the pulpits of LRCs, if it ever existed.

Inundated by religiously tinted myths about their own innocence tirelessly spawned from the pulpits of LRCs, believers are thus drilled to adopt the archaic nationalistic myths celebrating winners while showing no regard for the victims of their own national and religious narcissism. Incapacitated for guilt and forgiveness-seeking as the source of "healing of memories,"[42] they incline towards victimizing (*we are always the victims*) and infantilizing (*others are always to blame*) political programs, which are always, without fail, of nationalistic provenance in our region. Instead of being *experts on forgiveness and reconciliation* at the sociopolitical stage, they become *experts on hate and revenge*.

Through them, the abuse of religious symbols in LRCs—preferred means of homogenization by fear of others—creeps into the sociopolitical sphere. Instead of promoting *symbolic universal togetherness*, religious symbols are used for the application of "diabolical violence of the particular"[43]: demarcation, intimidation or exercising dominance over people of other religions or ethnicities. Of course, all of this is fanning the flames of hatred, and the religious hatred is unmatched in its shine!

Furthermore, religious peace makers or religiously inspired social reformers are not promoted as role models for believers in LRCs, but rather *warrior* saints, always an effective tool for closing ranks and inciting hatred against people of other religious and national affiliations. This is the reason why believers are far from being at the forefront of the processes of reconciliation and forgiveness.

---

40. Cf. Metz, *Politička teologija*, 1–320.
41. Adorno, *Negative Dialectics*, 17.
42. Cf. Accattolli, "Kad Papa traži oproštenje," 1–168.
43. Cf. Šarčević, "Totalitarizam, teologija i simboli," 87–97.

> In short: *The suppression of a new culture of remembrance in the religious sphere paves the way for the suppression of a new culture of remembrance in the sociopolitical sphere and vice versa!*

Social Solidarity

Reverberations of the withering social solidarity in transitional societies defined by unbridled social injustice are also felt in LRCs.

Inoculated against social ethics and the responsibility for an actual community, while pathologically reducing moral theology to sexuality, associated with spiritualism and liturgism, LRC leaders bring the issues of ethnicity within the realms of religion, rather than the burning social challenges. Since they give up on realizing their faith in the fullness of life, it mutates into its rhetorical, broken, and decadent surrogate in the social sphere. Indeed, superseded by ethnic concerns, open advocacy for social justice provokes accusations of "turning left" and betraying an ethnic group or a nation.

Obsessed with acquiring financial and material possessions for LRCs, with which they identify to such an extent that they accept gifts even from the public creators of social injustice, LRC leaders lose their freedom of announcement, the audacity to prophetically stand up against social injustice while publically and unequivocally condemning those responsible.[44] They do sometimes endeavor to restore some credibility by promoting humanitarian work within LRCs. But suppressing the effects of social injustice cannot substitute for confronting their causes.

Growing in faith stripped entirely of its social aspect or partially reduced to charitable activity, believers in LRCs are prepared to endorse political programs whose lack of receptiveness towards social challenges—causes but sometimes even the consequences of social injustice—conceal not the resoundingly declared ideological concerns but the well-guarded and profiteering economic crimes.

---

44. See Kristić, "Etička konkretnost objave," 393–410.

Now social awareness of believers in the sociopolitical sphere is further thwarted by the long-standing practice of nontransparent management in LRCs and not only in relation to believers but also donors, which often include municipalities and the state. Of course, it is always handed to the LRC leaders. Moreover, the LRC personnel often see their social rights trampled by LRC leaders.

This all serves the purpose of preparing believers for tolerating all forms of financial nontransparency, corruption, and social injustice.

In short: *The suppression of social awareness in the religious sphere paves the way for the suppression of social awareness in the sociopolitical sphere, and vice versa!*

Partnership between a Man and a Woman

The inability of transitional societies to respond positively to the challenges of transition is further aggravated by their insistence on ideological control and exclusion of women from the sociopolitical sphere. Failing to see and use the believing potential of women, LRCs in transitional societies behave in a fairly similar way.

As prisoners of theological constructs and devotions motivated by distrust or even hatred towards women, the LRC leaders prevent women from shaping different aspects of life in LRCs on an equal footing with men. Though often better educated than men, both in terms of economics and theology, women rarely get appointed in pastoral, economic or social councils in LRCs. Even the absence of any vitality and creativity in LRCs fails to prevent the exclusion of women. Of course, all of this is reinforced by the fact that leaders in LRC are most assuredly always men.

Having no opportunity to get to fully appreciate the believing potential of women in LRCs, believers are thus prepared to accept the exclusion of women from political, economic, and education structures, unaware of their innate democratic potential.

In short: *The suppression of the believing potential of women in religious sphere paves the way for the suppression of the democratic potential of women in sociopolitical sphere and vice versa!*

Cooperation for the Common Good

Corrupting *obsession with the state* as the source of their disorientation in the pluralistic society prevents religious communities in transitional societies from seeing the voluntary sector as a privileged place of witnessing faith. The desire for privileges suppresses the will to serve, causing LRC leaders to distrustfully close the door on the third sector.

Shifting the focus of believers onto the state and political parties as the sole guarantors of the survival of faith prevents the third sector from being recognized as the appropriate place where faith, as the responsibility for the whole world, is put into practice. In fact, the engagement of LRC members in the third sector would bring to the fore the suppressed aspects of the identity of believers, such as environmental awareness, living their faith in authenticity and integrity.

This would open up the opportunity for LRCs to exchange their submissive dependence on the state and political parties with the autonomous subjectivity in civil society, not only on account of its social desirability but also because the catharsis of believers would undoubtedly lead to the flourishing of vitality and creativity in LRC, and of course their capacity for democratic political socialization whose birthplace *is* civil society!

The summary of the discussion above would be the following—*unchecked power in religious communities paves the way for uncontrolled power in sociopolitical sphere and vice versa!*—leading us to conclude—*without true democratization of religious communities there will be no true democratization of society, and vice versa!*

Now we will explore a roughly outlined thesis on LRCs in the region as one of the key levers of political socialization of non-democratic political culture, providing a critical insight into the theological confrontations with certain politicians and political practices in the region, all the more valuable on account of their rarity.

Mutual interdependence of the development of subjectivity of believers rooted in LRCs, and the development of their civic and political subjectivity in terms of their values and focus indicates that every theological criticism of a political figure or a certain political practice will be wide of the mark unless—which is mainly not the case— it relates to practical efforts on building the democratic political culture, and primarily through the *democratization* of life in LRCs which, if *democratized*, would become paragons of democratic political socialization. But this is impossible to achieve without a parallel process of the *democratization* of religious communities in general.

More important than criticizing the individual *products* of nondemocratic political culture through a political figure or certain political practice—though this should not be approached separately—would be to critically confront the *workshops* of nondemocratic political culture, including LRCs as the leading ones. Of course, not only because nondemocratic political culture has for centuries bred all sorts of replicas of dismal political figures and practices in our region, but also because the nondemocratic political culture ensures them unreserved and unstinting popular support.

In fact, without a democratic shift in LRCs, especially in a society marked by desecularization—Bosnia and Herzegovina being the case in point—any attempt at breaking off with the nondemocratic political culture, which is the key requirement for its democratic consolidation, will be hard to imagine.

All the more reason for theological circles not to overlook their primary (though not the only one) responsibility when criticizing politics, i.e., scathing denunciation and suppression of mechanisms through which religious communities produce and endorse nondemocratic political culture, thus striking a happy medium between religious authenticity and social utility. In other words, instead of sending out moralizing dictates to the world, they should work on self-reflection as an authentic contribution to the healing of society.

Provided they decide to go down that road, the religious communities in the region are facing up to the challenges of democratizing LRCs, including the development of new pastoral forms, primarily *social* and *political*, only to be embarked upon following an in-depth research of life in LRCs.

At any rate, embracing their own *democratization* at all levels is the only way religious communities can join the ranks of sociopolitical agents resisting political and closely related congregational immaturity that consumes our region.

Of course, this is not to suggest that religious communities should now become ideological servants of democracy as they used to be in other sociopolitical systems in the past. On the contrary, by absorbing the positive aspects of democracy, rooted in religion though often fighting it, religious communities should be its critical friends, insistently encouraging theoretical questioning into the causes of its failures and practical process of its humanization despite all the efforts at "mythicizing democracy"![45]

III. POSTMETAPHYSICAL TURNAROUND OF RELIGIOUS SPHERE

As indicated earlier, the third part of this discussion will be focused on providing an answer—of course in terms of a thesis open for critical examination and scrutiny—to the question on the key obstacle or, to put it affirmatively, the key precondition for religious communities in Bosnia and Herzegovina to revive their potential for socialization of democratic political culture beyond politicization of religion and religionization of politics based on ethnic identity, and offer a concrete contribution to political liberation of man, as outlined on the final pages of *The Crucified God* by J. Moltmann.

Indeed, we are convinced that studying the predominant models of political socialization in LRCs has in a very specific way prepared us for this.

---

45. Cf. Sobrino, "Kritika današnjih demokracija," 39–54.

Metaphysical Mentality as a Fundamental Cause of the Instrumentalization of Religion for Political Slavery of Man Based on the Violent Configuration of the Religious Sphere

If we take a closer look at the analyzed mechanisms of political socialization in LRCs, unfortunately predominantly focused on the establishment and preservation of nondemocratic (or rather explicitly antidemocratic) mentality, and not only in the religious sphere but also in the political sphere, we will find out just to what extent the configuration of religion in our regional transitional societies is marked by violence; in fact, it is precisely this violence that binds them together.

But we don't want to stop at that and simply state that the violent configuration of religion in our context prevents religions from being agents of political liberation of man but elaborate it further with two interconnected claims. First, the violent configuration of religion in our context conceals the servitude of religions to the metaphysical mentality. Second, it is this metaphysical mentality that is responsible for political slavery in our region, both in terms of religion and politics.

In a nutshell, the bottom line to this is a deeply ingrained conviction that religion (including the truth of religion), whether it be Catholicism, Orthodox Christianity or Islam, is a permanently established objective givenness (*positum*), timeless and spaceless, only to be indisputably admired and—the key element at issue here—blindly followed in all aspects of their private and sociopolitical life, including the principles and laws derived from that permanently established objective givenness by the religious leaders as its sole guardians and interpreters.

Consequently it's about a concept of religion that eliminates every form of human freedom, primarily the freedom of critical thinking and challenging, of dialogue and pondering in general, as something redundant and disturbing. Moreover, in this conception even *divine* God, i.e., God beyond our *will to power*, becomes redundant and disturbing. For what is the ultimate purpose of the divine God—the question is well put—if religion (including the truth of religion) is a permanently established objective givenness to be guarded and applied to the present reality, even with the use of violence, which is of course completely legitimate since we are talking about the objective givenness of the divine origin?

Within such religion metaphysically conceived as a disposable kingdom of the eternal and unchanged truths, we need our neighbors and God himself solely as *mere material* or an exercise area for the monological and violent demonstration and application of the *sacred ground* whose monopolistic guarding and interpreting are assigned to us by the *divine providence*, seemingly solely for the purpose of *doing good* and *salvation* of others, rather than for the purpose of our sociopolitical privileges and advantages.

In other words: with these different manifestations of the violent configuration of religion in our postwar transitional context—and the above analyzed mechanisms of nondemocratic political socialization in LRCs are a glaring example of this—we are faced with alarming consequences of metaphysically conceived religiosity or deep-rootedness of metaphysical mentality in religion, not only in Christianity but also in Islam.

Of course, as might be assumed, following in the footsteps of Heidegger and Nietzsche, much in the vein of the postmodern Christian philosopher G. Vattimo, and Moltmann himself in *The Crucified God*, by metaphysics we mean the dominant form of Western thought and practice, specifically all theories that a system or an order of things wants to establish relying on a supposedly objective order understood as *positum*, established once and for all:

> Metaphysics is an idea, pride, and hope that we will meet incontestable, safeguarding but threatening "positum": the first principle, objectivity before which we should bow, in fact paternal authority imposing discipline . . .[46]

A clear indication that Moltmann, precisely through the metaphysical resistance to the reality or the concrete world, and for the purpose of remaining truthful to what is abstract and

---

46. Vattimo and Dotolo, *Dio: la possibilità buona*, 59.

objective as a reflex of ideological mystification, unveils the fundamental source of death of the positive potential of religion, even in the political sphere, is contained in his very succinct observation on the poisonous fruit of metaphysics in different aspects of religion, starting with fundamentalism—metaphysics is above all the thought and practice manifesting violence of the *safeguarding* foundation within which everything else, new or alien, is considered a threat to own survival:

> This lack of contact and blindness to the reality makes theology and churches increasingly obsolete . . . Fundamentalism fossilizes the Bible into an unquestionable authority. Dogmatism freezes living Christian tradition solid. The habitual conservatism of religion makes the liturgy inflexible, and Christian morality—often against its better knowledge and conscience—becomes a deadening legalism.[47]

But the same holds true for the political sphere, and in that context, instead of once and for all established objective givenness beyond the reach of critical questioning, there are, of course, *ethnic interests*, including the metaphysicized *civic virtues* which could serve the same purpose, as is blatantly evident in some cases of yearning for nationalistic and religious dominance hiding behind the commitment to those same civic principles in the sociopolitical sphere.

As might be expected, it is this spiritual kinship—slavery to metaphysical mentality—that serves as a foundation for the alliance between religion and politics in our postwar transitional context, and the alliance between the religionized politics and politicized or nationalized faith is nothing else but the opportunistic alliance between religious and political metaphysics, where the nationalistic and religious ghetto is a perfect reflex of this alliance at the level of a sociopolitical form, in the absence of any viable opportunities for establishing a sustainable Islamic, or Christian state, whether Catholic or Orthodox.

---

47. Moltmann, *Crucified God*, 2.

All things considered, in our transitional context, both in terms of politics and religion, we are enslaved by metaphysical mentality as the source of religious and political violence, but also by pernicious instrumentalization of religion for the purpose of establishing and maintaining the political enslavement of people, and this is precisely what humanity needs to free itself from if we are, as pointed out by the postmodern Christian philosopher G. Vattimo, to recognize the positive opportunities for promotion of humaneness in the postmodern world as it relates to our context of postwar and transitional traumas:

> It will be impossible for thought to live positively through that true and proper post-metaphysical era called post-modernity, as long as man and being are construed metaphysically and platonically, in terms of solid structures that would assign thought and existence the task of "founding" itself, of settling (through logic and ethics) in the realm of nonbeing by reflecting itself entirely in the mythicization of strong structures in every field of experience.[48]

The fact that Moltmann himself, in his own peculiar way, came to the same conclusion in *The Crucified God* as early as 1972, is a strong paradigmatic indication of the quality and prophetic profile of his theology.

The Post-Metaphysical Configuration of Religions as a Precondition for Their Transformation into Agents of Political Liberation of Human Being

That Christianity in its origins is not and can never be a metaphysical construct if it is to preserve *a grain of mustard seed* of authenticity, essentially constitutes the subversive message of both Moltmann's *The rucified God* and, looking back at the recent Catholic tradition, the Second Vatican Council.

---

48. Vattimo, *La fine della modernità*, 20.

Indeed, precisely on account of disclosing this subversive message, both *The Crucified God* and the Second Vatican Council are quite often seen as *devil's work*; but regardless of this, if Muslims and Jews do not want Islam and Judaism to function as religion-clad totalitarianisms or fundamentalisms, they will have to embark on an urgent quest to find that subversive message within the Islamic and Jewish traditions, for:

> The talk about God does not constitute the stewardship of an estate but the quest for God in deserts and oases of life. The talk about God does not constitute administration of inheritance we are entitled to, but the process of incessantly making new, always vulnerable, forever precarious, never safeguarded discoveries. For God reveals but also withdraws himself; there is "the permanent resurrection of faith from the grave of unbelief" as formulated by Karl Rahner, since faith can also mean "enduring God's silence."[49]

Now, below is a brief outline of what the post-metaphysical Christianity would look like if stripped of the *straightjacket* of metaphysical mentality (analogous outlines should be conceived for Islam and Judaism) or unreligious Christianity—as G. Vattimo would put it, including some of the leading Christian theologians of the twentieth century such as D. Bonhoeffer and J. Moltmann—finally achieving its original antimetaphysical mission, or rather its fate; in other words Christianity in its unique, though never once and for all established authentic form:

> We must constantly try to reveal the sense and meaning of gospel also from the perspective of others. It does not suffice to keep repeating the old patterns of faith, even when they really mean something to us—which in any case is neither self-evident nor once and for all guaranteed. Without this perspective-changing ability, pastoral care won't be possible in the future or even now. But this change of perspective is in a sense easier than it might seem. For, on the one hand, it is clear that we can take

---

49. Bucher, *Die Provokation der Krise*, 193.

only some specific perspectives, never all of them. On the other hand, there are more than one perspective on gospel in us. Practically nobody lives in only one world any more, we all inhabit a multitude of worlds. The contrast between this multitude of worlds and our (perhaps rather happily inhabited) church world should not be concealed; it is essential that we in fact let it be creative. Those who don't understand anything about "the modern world" will not understand anything about "the church in the modern world," nor decipher the gospel of that world, since it cannot be revealed by taking the people of that world as the starting point. And this is the task of the church and pastoral care overall: the church shall become God's people when it reveals the gospel in word and deed based on human life, and liberates life based on the gospel. This is the interpenetration of life and teachings as the principle of pastoral work of the Second Vatican Council. It indeed represents a new structuring of the system of religious meaning itself, since it is set in the horizon of contemporary human existence and its constitutive reference framework for action. But the necessity of external perspective, a permanent change of perspective, entails the following as well: the church has to keep relearning what gospel means today. Although possessing the authentic history of revelation of faith though Scripture and tradition, the church today is still obliged to undertake such revelations. And the pastoral care primarily represents these revelation events, in word and deed.[50]

Unfortunately, Christianity has lived its history so far exclusively in the form of "metaphysical misunderstanding of the original meaning of the New Testament message"[51] (M. Heidegger), applying also to our postwar transitional context, and including Islam as well, even more so given the susceptibility of crisis-prone and border regions such as ours to all forms of metaphysical thinking and practice.

50. Bucher, *Die Provokation der Krise*, 40–41.
51. Vattimo, *Jenseits des Christentums*, 179.

In fact, what we have here is—by way of illustration—a fatal falsification of Jesus's claim, "I am the way and the truth and the life" (John 14:6) by the church at the sociopolitical and church-politics level, whereby the truth is put before the way with horrifying consequences.

The Christian truth thus becomes an objectivistic or even apodictic truth. A truth in our absolute possession and scope, requiring neither God nor neighbor for its revelation, or rather needing no revelation since it is everlasting and inalterable. Such conception of truth also subsumes forgetting our own discardedness, or in other words, our own historicity and createdness, and above all our own mortality, and with it the original addressedness by God and the world.

For this reason, Christianity has very often been a religious ideology rather than history, since every objectivistic truth—and above all the objectivistic theology resting on the mere claim on God's love, rather than on personal witnessing closely related to the humble listening to God and solidary listening to our neighbor—is ideologically motivated. The objectivistic truth isolates us from the concrete fight to defend human dignity of modern people, sacralizing inhuman situations. It produces *faith without discipleship* and truth without (or rather against) solidarity, the very essence of Christianity as ideology.

Metaphysics or church Platonism (including, of course, religious Platonism in general) finding its source in theoretical certainty—the primacy of the truth over the way as a solidary feeling for others—and seeking to dispose of everything (even God), primarily represents the defense against "the anxiety of the deed"[52] or discipleship of Jesus, or in wholly concrete terms the necessity of reinventing Christianity as a free, risky, and rewarding response to the incarnation of God or kenosis, which is not a command but an offer or an appeal directed towards not only Christians but all people.

An escape from the creative response to kenosis is compensated by neurotic and reactive defense of the status quo and

---

52. Žižek, "Za teološko–političku obustavu etičkog," 267.

absolutizing one vision or potentiality of Christianity inextricably linked to different forms of violence, which to a shocking degree define the history of Christianity as well as of Islam. Without the incessant incarnation or kenosis in concrete time and space—at all levels and in all places—church will inevitably slip into a sacral ghetto, being susceptible and attractive solely to totalitarian and fundamentalistically formatted political projects.

IV. CONTEXTUAL IMPLEMENTATION OF THE FUNDAMENTAL PROGRAM OF *THE CRUCIFIED GOD*

Now, what would be the concrete implications of the discussion above for the configuration of religion in our postwar transitional context? What concrete shape would Catholicism, Orthodox Christianity and Islam in our region assume if stripped of their metaphysical mentality as the source of political and religious destructiveness? What should be a concrete setup of postmetaphysical Catholicism, Orthodox Christianity or Islam in our region affected by a series of postwar and transitional traumas? Or does this sound rather blasphemous by and of itself? On the whole, what would be the first step in terms of making a shift from the metaphysical towards postmetaphysical mentality in the religious sphere in our region?

In other words, what would constitute the concrete and contextual implementation of the fundamental program of *The Crucified God* by J. Moltmann for religions in Bosnia and Herzegovina (and our region in general), whereby we primarily mean the kenotic and solidary descent of religions into *the present situations of the crucified God*, and the *present vicious circles of death*, or rather embracing *the cross of modernity*?

First, the religious institutions should reflect deeply on their complicity with the last war and *the vicious circles of death* of the postwar transitional hopelessness, for only in that agonizing cathartic confrontation with their dark side can they become aware of and own up to all the fatal religious and sociopolitical ramifications of their metaphysical setup and practices.

Of course, the first concrete sign of this confession would be the departure from corrupting fixation on the state, and the political and nationalistic elites in positions of power, and acknowledgement that they do not hold the *metaphysical patent* over what it means to be a Christian (Catholic or Orthodox) or a Muslim in our current postwar and transitional context while keeping in mind that this fixation on politics is certainly one of the prime reasons for the loss of credibility of religious institutions, not only at the regional but also at the global level:

> Seeking to benefit from politics, religion tends to lose all credibility and efficiency, sometimes, as a punishment for its unbelief, stooping even below the credibility and efficiency of politics itself. As we are witnesses to this on a daily basis, a better option seems to be aligning with savvy politics rather than the fanaticized religion.[53]

Second, in searching for an answer as to what it means to be a Christian or a Muslim in concrete terms in this region, religious communities should turn to the solidary observation of people who are left at the mercy of postwar transitional traumas defending their vulnerable human dignity, since the answer to the question on authentic Christianity and Islam in our region rests with such people rather than with the privileged political, economic, religious or cultural elites.

Programmatically said: beyond the metaphysical mentality, as the source of violent configuration of the entire religious sphere, and the fatal instrumentalization of religion for the establishment and preservation of political slavery of man, religious institutions in our postwar transitional context are facing a challenge of (kenotic) shifting away from the utopias of nationalistic and religious ghettos towards the heterotopias of the postwar transitional traumas, or in concrete terms, towards the places where people,

---

53. Mardešić, *Svjedočanstva o mirotvorstvu*, 52.

surrendered to their postwar transitional troubles, fight for their threatened human dignity.

Only then and on the basis of practical solidarity, knowing no religious or national boundaries, with the people whose dignity is threatened in the turmoil of transition, will the religious institutions be able to experience and uncover what it means to be an authentic Christian or a Muslim in our area and our time, whereby it should not be surprising that humaneness is *imposed* as the criterion of authentic religiosity rather than of the abstract and theoretical orthodoxy:

> Inhumaneness is greater blasphemy than unbelief, and since it comes from the congregational circles of the rich and powerful, this is exactly where the healing should begin. To acknowledge God is easy, but it's far more demanding and harder to help people in distress. And Jesus Christ came exactly for the latter, while all religions have always preached faith in God and offered sacrifices to him.[54]

Moreover, religious communities will finally escape the temptation of authoritarian and forceful imposition of their monological and unhistorical vision of Christianity or Islam onto others and the unquestionable explications of the Christian or Islamic principles in the area of politics, ethics or economy. In other words: religious institutions shall recover their authenticity, inevitably losing their political power while gaining spiritual authority, only if they entirely expose themselves to the postwar transitional heterotopias, i.e., the places of the concrete struggle for human dignity, and this despite our tendency to turn our back on these heterotopias, and not least because they unveil the deception and destroy our conceited religious triumphalism, both in terms of our relationship to God and the sheer magnificence of our christianness or muslimness.

Once they are *baptized* or invented against the backdrop of solidary deliverance to the postwar transitional heterotopias, only the (institutional) setup, (theological) discourse, and (pastoral)

54. Mardešić, *Rascjep u svetome*, 687.

practice of the religious institutions will be entitled to religious authenticity and—far more important—humaneness:

> The treasure of own message cannot be revived without others and that which is opposed to their incarnation. Those who are not apprenticed to the existential problems of the people of the day will not be able to teach them faith. Without prospects of their incarnation, the church will not be able to develop historically relevant notion of the truth of their faith.[55]

Of course, this would also mean that religious institutions no longer play the role of (metaphysical) guardians of mythicized *ethnic identity*, but in a reconciled and reverse way keep showing concern for demystified *ethnic values*, only now as the guardians of humaneness, all the more so since ethnic identity, both as a cultural and political horizon, can only be preserved and maintained in such a way.

Rather than the mythicized ethnic identity, only *humaneness*, concrete and tied to a specific time and place, and defined through the dialogical process, can be the principle of the constitution and activity of religious institutions, provided that they do not want to be a reflex and a medium of a religion-clad totalitarianism or fundamentalism.

No matter how paradoxical it may sound, we might conclude that the positive religious and cultural, as well as sociopolitical factor in our or any other region in the world cannot be metaphysically *strong* but postmetaphysically *weak* and thus solidary religions, i.e., religions resembling a fragile Christianity preferred, for example, not by a heretic but by a French bishop named A. Rouet, which is a further indication that sociopolitical powerlessness, a constant fear tormenting religious communities, is the key precondition for religious and spiritual power that no longer finds its origin in the power of the sociopolitically *strong* and privileged, which is the source of its violence, but in the powerlessness of the sociopolitically *weak* and underprivileged, which is the source of

---

55. Sander, "Die Zeichen der Zeit," 101–2.

its nonviolence and the ability to restore human dignity to those downtrodden, including the oppressors provided that they let themselves be affected by it:

> I long for a church which dares show its fragility, vulnerability and powerlessness. The gospel says that Christ dared show hunger and asked Zacchaeus for some food. The church today sometimes gives the impression that it needs nothing and that people have nothing to give it. I long for a church which stands loudly and courageously by each man and does not conceal its fragility, sinfulness, ignorance and occasional perplexity . . . In short, a church tormented by false teachings and lack of trust in people and in dialogue with them.[56]

Of course the precondition to fulfilling the vision of the weak church or more generally weak religions in our region—getting back to the fundamental insight of Moltmann's *Crucified God*—is an agonizing but a saving departure from the indifferent God, an ideological or idolatrous aberration, coupled with the prospect of subversive encounter with the empathic God gracing the face and the fate of the crucified *rebel* from Galilee, all the more so since the essential feature of *our God*, whether it be indifference or active compassion, discloses itself in concrete terms in our every thought or practical endeavor, even when we are not aware of it, determining decisively not only our own psychological but also our common sociopolitical reality:

> God who cannot suffer is poorer than any man. For a God who is incapable of suffering is a being who cannot be involved. Suffering and injustice do not affect him. And because he is so completely insensitive, he cannot be affected or shaken by anything. He cannot weep, for he has no tears. But the one who cannot suffer cannot love either. He is also a loveless being. Aristotle's God cannot love; he can be loved by all non-divine beings by virtue of his perfection and beauty and in this way draw them to him. The "unmoved Mover" is a "loveless Beloved." If

---

56. No coincidence, this quotation from "La chance d'un christianisme fragile" by A. Rouet was found in Mardešić, "Dnevnik," 170.

he is the ground of the love (*eros*) of all things for him (*causa prima*) and at the same time his own cause (*causa sui*), he is the beloved who is in love with himself; a Narcissus in a metaphysical degree: *Deus incurvatus in se* . . . Finally, a God who is only omnipotent is in himself an incomplete being, for he cannot experience helplessness and powerlessness. Omnipotence can indeed be longed for and worshipped by helpless men, but omnipotence is never loved; it is only feared. What sort of being, then, would be a God who was only "almighty"? He would be a being without experience, a being without destiny and a being who is loved by no one. A man who experiences helplessness, a man who suffers because he loves, a man who can die, is therefore a richer being than an omnipotent God who cannot suffer, cannot love and cannot die. Therefore for a man who is aware of the riches of his own nature in his love, his suffering, his protest and his freedom, such a God is not a necessary and supreme being, but a highly dispensable and superfluous being.[57]

Nevertheless, a rather clear and almost unrivaled, though in no way self-explanatory or simple, testimony to the understanding that turning to the weak God, to the God on the other side of indifference, to the God capable of suffering, the only one that can help us precisely on that account, as D. Bonhoeffer rightly concluded long time ago in his Gestapo cell, is contained in Moltmann's letter written to Rahner after Rahner's death, since it was only then that he found Rahner's critique of the *theology of the crucified God*, which for Moltmann as well as for us, ends in Rahner's equally shocking and terrifying words that God is in a consolatory sense a nonsuffering God.

Now, to conclude this discussion, we will take an excerpt from this letter, a curious specimen of the history of theology, containing, in our humble opinion, the key to eliminating the metaphysical inhibition of religions in our region through their servitude to religious nationalism, for we are all, whether personally or

57. Moltmann, *Crucified God*, 229–30.

communally (even if only tending towards it), the very reflection of the kind of God we worship:

> I find no connection between consolation and apathy and therefore find no way into your experience of God and self. Of course God entered into our history of suffering in a divine way; he was not subjected to it against his will. For the theologians of the early church there was only the involuntary suffering of creation and the essential apathy of the Godhead. But there is a third form of suffering, the voluntary suffering of love for the beloved and in the beloved. That God does not suffer as finite creatures suffer does not mean that he is incapable of suffering in any way. God is capable of suffering because he is capable of love. His being is mercy. I developed this at length in my book *The Crucified God*. An impossible God is capable of neither love nor feeling. Empathy is impossible for such a God. So such a God is not in a position to console people either. One can only console when one shares another's feelings. And one can only share another's feelings in one has empathy. And having empathy means being passible and not impassible. I cannot imagine an impassible God as a God who consoles in a personal sense. He seems to me to be as cold and as hard and unfeeling as cement.[58]

—Translated by Dragana Divković

---

58. Moltmann, *History and the Triune God*, 123.

BIBLIOGRAPHY

Accattolli, Luigi. *Kad Papa traži oproštenje: Svi mea culpa Ivana Pavla II*. Translated by Mate Križman. Split: Franjevački institut za kulturu mira, 2000.

Adorno, Theodor W. *Negative Dialectics*. Translated by A. B. Ashton. London: Routledge, 1973.

Baum, Gregory. "Crkva—za i protiv demokracije." *Jukić* 38/39 (2008/9) 17–27.

Bojić, Drago. "Večernji H–B list." *Svjetlo riječi* 349 (2012) 4–5.

Bucher, Rainer, ed. *Die Provokation der Krise: Zwölf Fragen und Antworten zur Lage der Kirche*. Würzburg: Echter, 2005

Dahrendorf, Ralph. *Razmatranja o revoluciji u Europi*. Translated by Ivan Prpić. Zagreb: Antibarbarus, 1996.

Dugalić, Vladimir. "Politička traganja Crkve u Hrvatskoj (1989–2007)." *Bogoslovska smotra* 2 (2007) 483–539.

Frank, Sejmon L. "Rušenje idola." *Europski glasnik* 13 (2008) 771–828.

Fuchs, Gotthard, and Andreas Lienkamp, eds. *Visionen des Konzils. 30 Jahre Pastoralkonstitution "Die Kirche in der Welt von heute"*. Schriften des Instituts für Christliche Sozialwissenschaften 36. Münster: Lit, 1997.

Habermas, Jürgen, and Joseph Ratsinger. "Dijalektika sekularizacije—O umu i religiji." Translated by Nataša Medved. *Europski glasnik* 12 (2007) 185–208.

Hölderlin, Friedrich. *Gedichte*. Edited by Gerhard Kurz in collaboration with Wolfgang Braungart. Stuttgart: Phillip Reclam, 2000.

Kristić, Alen. "Etička konkretnost objave—Poticaj za kontekstualno čitanje 'Etike.'" In *Etika*, by Dietrich Bonhoeffer, 393–410. Rijeka: Ex libris, 2009.

———. *Religija i moć*. Sarajevo: Rabic, 2009.

———. *Tiranija religijskog: Ogledi o religijskom bezboštvu*. Sarajevo: Rabic, 2014.

———. "Vjerske institucije u BiH: Govor 'razrokosti'?" In *Hrvati u BiH: Ustavni položaj, kulturni razvoj i nacionalni identitet*, edited by Ivan Markešić, 167–201. Zagreb: Centar za demokraciju i pravo "Miko Tripalo," 2010.

Küng, Hans. *Svjetski ethos za svjetsku politiku*. Translated by Berislav Baotić. Zagreb: Intercon, 2007.

Marasović, Špiro. "Demokratska očekivanja od Crkve u Hrvatskoj između minimalizma i maksimalizma." *Diacovensia* 1 (2002) 23–70.

Mardešić, Željko. "Dnevnik: između sjećanja i traženja novoga." *Nova Prisutnost* 2 (2004) 167–84.

———. *Rascjep u svetome*. Zagreb: Kršćanska sadašnjost, 2007.

———. *Svjedočanstva o mirotvorstvu*. Zagreb: Kršćanska sadašnjost, 2002.

Máté-Tóth, András, and Pavel Mikluščák. *Nicht wie Milch und Honig: unterwegs zu einer Pastoraltheologie Ost (Mittel) Europas; Gott nach dem Kommunismus*. Ostfildern: Schwabenverlag, 2000.

Metz, Johannes Baptist. *Politička teologija*. Translated by Željko Čekolj. Zagreb: Kršćanska sadašnjost, 2004.

Moltmann, Jürgen. *The Crucified God: The Cross of Christ as the Foundation and Criticism of Christian Theology*. Translated by R. A. Wilson and John Bowden. London: SCM, 2001.

———. *History and the Triune God: Contributions to Trinitarian Theology*. Translated by John Bowden. New York: Crossroad, 1992.

Pavić, Željko. *Arhonti bitka: Pokus filozofije vjere*. Rijeka: Ex libris, 2009.

Queiruga, Andrés Torres. *La Chiesa oltre la democrazia*. Translated by F. Sudati. Molfetta: La Meridiana, 2004.

Sander, Hans-Joachim. "Die Zeichen der Zeit—Die Entdeckung des Evangeliums in den Konflinkten der Gegenwart." In *Visionen des Konzils. 30 Jahre Pastoralkonstitution "Die Kirche in der Welt von heute"*, edited by Gotthard Fuchs and Andreas Lienkamp, 85–102. Schriften des Instituts für Christliche Sozialwissenschaften 36. Münster: Lit, 1997.

Šarčević, Ivan. "Totalitarizam, teologija i simboli—Sakralizirana politika i nacionalizirana vjera: primjer Bosne i Hercegovine." *Nova prisutnost* 1 (2010) 87–97.

Šimac, Neven. "Kršćanin u politici i suvremenoj Europi." *Bogoslovska smotra* 2 (2007) 541–61.

Sobrino, Jon. "Kritika današnjih demokracija i putovi ka njihovu humaniziranju s gledišta biblijsko-isusovske tradicije." *Jukić* 38/39 (2008/9) 39–54.

Vattimo, Gianni. *Jenseits des Christentums: Gibt es eine Welt ohne Gott?* Translated by Martin Pfeiffer. Munich: Carl Hanser, 2004.

———. *La fine della modernità*. Milan: Garzanti, 1999.

Vattimo, Gianni, and Carmelo Dotolo. *Dio: la possibilità buona*. Soveria Mannelli: Rubbettino, 2009.

Volf, Miroslav. *Trinität und Gemeinschaft: Eine ökumenische Ekklesiologie*. Neukirchen-Vluyn: Neukirchener, 1996.

Vujadinović, Dragica. "Civilno društvo i politička kultura." *Filozofska istraživanja* 109 (2008) 21–33.

Vujčić, Vladimir. *Politička kultura demokracije*. Osijek: Panliber, 2001.

———. "Politička kultura i politička struktura: odnos političke kulture, strukture i demokracije (I)." *Politička misao* 36/1 (1999) 113–39.

———. "Politička kultura i politička struktura: odnos političke kulture, strukture i demokracije (II)." *Politička misao* 36/2 (1999) 144–57.

———. "Tipologija političke kulture." *Politička misao* 35/4 (1998) 98–131.

Žižek, Slavoj. "Za teološko-političku obustavu etičkog." In *Bog na mukama/ obrati apokalipse*, by Slavoj Žižek and Boris Gunjević. Translated by Roman Karlović. Rijeka: Ex libris, 2008.

4

Theological Discourse in the Vicious Circle of Apathy

—Entoni Šeperić

INTRODUCTION

The Christian hermeneutics of history as history of salvation (of the chosen ones) has found its contextual expression in Balkan nationalistic ideologies and politicized religions. Our national pantheons are filled with demigods that feed on the epic patriotism of martyrdom and the infallibility of the nation. There are, indeed, many contextual factors and unconcealed ideological traits enabling this disturbing conflation of individual and communal bigotry that feeds on religion. The sacrificial appetites of national deities constantly demand the production of ever new identity markers, to which religion readily lends its metaphors and language. Ideological appropriations of Christianity—of its core symbols, subjects, and structures—are so interdependent and interwoven with popular religion and its attendant narratives of pride and nationhood, that they have become almost identical and inseparable. The thought-forms and rhetoric of rivalry, which go hand in hand with this sense of national superiority—all too common traits of any *Christus Victor* ecclesiology—have become well established facts in our postwar local and regional church life and theology. Creative and subversive domestic theological voices are rare; even if they appear, they are easily relegated to the margins of social and church life and made virtually unimportant.

With this paper I move toward a contextual redefinition of what it means to practice theology within the context of denial of mass murders and genocide. I first offer some contextual and biographical underpinnings by recounting my engagement with Moltmann's theology of the cross, which will serve to emphasize the importance of individual experiential frameworks in theology. In the second part, I venture to explore the possibilities of new and contrite theological metaphors in our quest for a contextual theology informed by full awareness of mass murders and genocide, of victims and their suffering. I find one of these possibilities in engagement with the article of Jesus's descent into hell of the Apostles' Creed and explore a set of theologically pertinent questions through critical engagement with the theology of Jesus's descent in the work of Hans Urs von Balthasar. I also argue that contemporary theological discourse has become constitutionally deaf to the terrors of mass murders and genocide, suggesting that this deafness marks an important shift or change in the social locus of Christianity and theology in Europe and America.

JÜRGEN MOLTMANN: THEOLOGY AS A BIOGRAPHY

The fact that Moltmann's radical theology of the cross provokes reactions even four decades since its publication, and in seemingly very different historical contexts, probably does not suffice to give it the status of a theological classic. Yet, a large number of theological monographs and articles which build on and critically engage with its principal themes and theological questions are certainly a sufficient testimony that Moltmann's work has struck a personal chord not only with its supporters, but also with its critics. Moltmann's work is essentially a theological biography. It is not only written in a biographical manner, but, also, any reaction to it was always and is essentially—*autobiographical*. This personal quality is the primary reason why his book stands out as a landmark in the theology of the twentieth century.

In his introduction to the essays collected in this book, by analyzing the impact of *The Crucified God* in a broader context, Moltmann points out the importance of different hermeneutical contexts for a correct understanding of its main themes. Starting with the recognition of how he was affected by his own situation, or the context out of which his book was written, he approaches the context of its effects and emphasizes that a particular work of theology does not belong exclusively to its own *kairos*, but *also* carries meaning into the contextual horizons of readers who are, in turn, affected by the personal experiences of its author. But before I venture to talk about the context of my personal resonance with *The Crucified God*, I will consider the experience that stands at the roots of his theological discourse.

The Crucified God is undoubtedly written from the perspective of a shattered existence. It reveals the perspective of an existential landslide, a life beaten down and almost defeated by the excruciating realities of war. Moltmann's work is deeply imbued with the authority and normativity of the suffering subject, which has only recently become theologically important for Catholic theology with the work of Johann Baptist Metz, who is Moltmann's contemporary and compatriot. Therefore, if it is meaningful to talk about Moltmann's theology as carrying out a particular task, then the task is in its effects akin to that of Metz's project of "provocative anamnesis" in a pluralistic society, and in its own stimulus perhaps completely identical with it.[1] It is essentially a theological biography that does not claim the authority of the speaker outside her ability to speak about God incoherently, mumbling out of being personally struck by the question of theodicy. Such a theology rarely slips into the apathy of cold discourse, the pathos of

---

1. Cf. Metz, *Memoria passionis*.

nice wordings where everything is given beforehand and easily *materialized* in faith. On the contrary, it wrestles sincerely with the issues that derive their meaning from the contradictions of a torn and battered existence, and it is exactly this contradiction that holds its questions always open and unforgettable.

The burden and trauma of Moltmann's generation in the war and in postwar Germany represents the context out of which his theology of the cross arose as an attempt to get a hold of the life in faith and survive the apocalyptic horizon of the world. The crucial experiences for such a vision were lost youth and the feeling of utter betrayal, the horrors of mass murder and concentration camps, orgies of death and suppression of life. But none of that, certainly, was as disturbing and devastating as Moltmann's awareness that— by a twist of fate and contrary to his own will—he belonged to the generation of perpetrators, as well as his awareness that he carried the shame of the mass murder of Jews.

> In 1961 I walked through what was left of the death camp Majdanek by Lublin. I saw the children's shoes, the cut off hair, and I was overwhelmed by shame. And as I was walking alone through one of the camp streets I had a vision: I saw the murdered children walking towards me in the fog. Since then, I am convinced that there is a resurrection of the dead.[2]

But, theologically speaking, what did it mean to belong to the nation of perpetrators? The urgency of dealing with the issue gave birth to a new theological consciousness, and this "poorness" of theology appeared as if sentenced to aimless wandering through the aesthetic leisure of theological discourse, threatening to discard the concreteness of suffering by means of a compensation strategy to relativize personal responsibility. Faith and theology required room for the growing awareness that the guilt and shame should not only be felt, but that it was necessary to live with open questions if one is to accept full responsibility for his or her own theology, theology that is no longer able to provide comfort in the

---

2. See Moltman, "*The Crucified God* in Context," in this volume, 1–17.

bourgeois notion of Christ's death as forgiveness of *our sins*. It was no longer possible to maintain mere awareness of human suffering unaffected by pressing and documented horrors—*Christ has become a curse for us* (Gal 3:13).

> Wherever people are murdered, gassed, tortured or shot, the Crucified is among them . . . They are his people. They partake in his passion.[3]

Yet, is the suffering of those innocently killed *constitutive* for our experiential and interpretative Christian framework? And what are the consequences of such an insight for systematic theology, Christology, ecclesiology?

THEOLOGY OUT OF THE VICIOUS CIRCLE OF DEATH

The darkness of human suffering in history dramatically confronts Christianity and theology with a renewed question of God. It seems as if we as theologians have already slid into *mythical* consciousness, which is marked by efforts to minimize ethical indeterminacy, or to completely remove all uncomfortable questions that arise from the voiceless sighs of the victims. Under the layers of our theologically polished language lurks a disturbing awareness of the limits of possibility that after Srebrenica and Tomašica[4]—

---

3. Ibid., 6.

4. Srebrenica is a town and municipality in easternmost Bosnia and Herzegovina. It is known for the Srebrenica massacre in July 1995, which is deemed genocidal by the decision of the International Criminal Tribunal for the former Yugoslavia (ICTY). The killings of more than eight thousand civilians, mainly Bosniak men and boys, were perpetrated by the forces of the Bosnian Serb Army of Republika Srpska under the command of General Ratko Mladić. In April 1993, the United Nations declared the besieged enclave of Srebrenica a "safe area" under UN protection. However, in July 1995, UNPROFOR's soldiers in Srebrenica failed to prevent the town's capture by the Bosnian Serb Army of Republika Srpska and the subsequent massacre.

Tomašica is a village in the Prijedor municipality in northwestern Bosnia and Herzegovina. It is the site where, in August 2013, Bosnian authorities discovered one of the largest primary mass grave sites from the Bosnian war.

without irritation and shame—we can still talk about universal Christian salvation. With what intent could we honestly believe that our God-talk encompasses the vision and promise of great righteousness for those who suffer, or is it an empty talk, devoid of promise for them? It seems that adaptive deafness and endless relativization are able to endure the horrors that have shifted metaphysical boundaries of shame between human beings—*Your brother's blood cries out to me from the ground* (Gen 4:10).

Radical Christian faith, according to Moltmann, is to be unreservedly engaged in the experiential framework of the crucified God. "To make the cross a present reality in our civilization," Moltmann remarks, "means to put into practice the experience one has received of being liberated from fear for oneself; no longer to adapt oneself to this society, its idols and taboos, its imaginary enemies and fetishes; and in the name of him who was once the victim of religion, society and the state to enter into solidarity with the victims of religion, society and the state at the present day, in the same way as he who was crucified became their brother and their liberator."[5] If we want to take his remarks seriously, then we must talk about our own idols and taboos, our own hostile images and fetishes, and think through our own shares in this hostility.

Discussing theology from the devil's circles of death inevitably involves talk about political liberation; slavery inevitably involves talk about slave masters. An experiential hermeneutic of life in the shadow of the crucified one remains incomplete if it fails to be complemented by the appropriate political hermeneutics. This is to remind us that the sociopolitical dimension, however, is never lost in Hebrew and Christian messianism, and always remains the central expression of what it means to obey God.[6] But what is a political hermeneutics of faith under the aegis of a hermeneutics of innocence? Is it not precisely in the service of theological jus-

---

Exhumation activities in cooperation with the International Commission on Missing Persons (ICMP) started soon after the discovery, and it is believed that the site holds the remains of more than a thousand people.

5. Moltmann, *Crucified God*, 40.
6. See Ruether, *To Change the World*, 11.

tification of a *status quo*, a condition in which there is no courage to take a critical account of that caricature of Christian hope that is already secularized into a mere utopia? Regardless of whether we are talking about the real or imagined dilemma, the answer remains uncomfortably urgent, and almost paralyzing in its final consequences.

Speaking of the ways to the political liberation of mankind, Moltmann not only felt the pressure of this dilemma but also foreshadowed a possible way out: "The path of a theology of the cross that is critical of society goes between irrelevant Christian identity and social relevance without Christian identity."[7] His answer, therefore, set foot in the midst of a socio-critical theology of the cross. He observed that the political hermeneutics of faith includes a theoretical break with idols, taboos, imagined enmities, and self-justifications arising from the reality of a political religion, as well as practical advocacy for "others" who have become victims of the prevailing political religion in society. In other words, there are clear practical requirements set before any political theology seeking be a corrective to "non-situational" (abstract) theology.

In contrast with the sacrosanct character of our local theologies that arise from symbolic and real justification of our collective amnesia, out of the realm of denial and negation of mass murders and genocide, we must make our own choices between irrelevant Christian identity and social relevance without Christian identity. It is only within this framework that our contextual interest in the theology of the cross as the basis for criticism of Christian theology becomes comprehensible. It is the framework within which the talk about human suffering reverberates, along with the question of theodicy, in spite of various theological strategies to minimize or immunize the uneasiness caused by genuine human suffering through its subsequent transfer into the talk about a God who suffers. It is against this background—if I read correctly—that the caution and restraint of some contemporary political theologians (cf. Metz) from the talking of a God who suffers becomes understandable.

7. Moltmann, *Crucified God*, 324.

Theology—Descent into the Vicious Circles of Death

The codification of genuine human suffering into a theological table talk about the suffering God is tantamount to its theoretical overcoming and is without practical consequences for the transformation of the present or the construction of the future. The talk of the God who suffers is indeed to walk on the thin ice of innocuous theological complacency, and psychologically sustains our state of utmost remoteness and indifference concerning the actual suffering subject or its cause. Thus the theological codification of the talk of the God who suffers into theological-speculative overcoming of actual human suffering so easily transforms into a "stopper" for critical and practical engagement with its causes, which may also be theological in nature. From the perspective of pastoral care for the victims of violence, however, nothing is as repugnant as idle talk of the God who suffers as opposed to the concreteness of their loss and suffering. That only the suffering God can save us, as Bonhoeffer would put it, is not palpable outside the authority of the suffering subject, and has no meaning unless it is able to stand alongside the victim and withstand the agonizing psychological effects of a return question—"My God, my God, why have you forsaken me?" (Matt 27:46).

The tension between these two poles of Christian witness, along with the pregnant silence of horror that separates them, is marked by the awareness that salvation is a universal theme, the theme of humanity, or it is no theme at all. Yet, what it means practically to a mother who—almost twenty years after the crimes were committed near Prijedor[8]—still roams from one mass grave to another looking for the bones of her six brutally murdered children, surpasses all my theological ingenuity, so that even the audacity to appear before her so dangerously touches upon or indeed goes beyond the limits of shame which the crime has set in between us, even though—or perhaps precisely because—we could not or did

---

8. Prijedor is a city and municipality in northwestern Bosnia and Herzegovina. During the Bosnian war (1992–1995), the area near the city housed the infamous Omarska, Keraterm, and Trnopolje concentration camps. The Prijedor massacre refers to numerous war crimes committed during the war, and it constitutes the second largest massacre commited by the forces of the Bosnian Serb Army of Republika Srpska.

not want to do anything to prevent it. Instead of renouncing our right to speak, additionally warned by the possibility that the perpetrators of that horrible crime may have confessed an untroubled faith in the merit of their repugnant work for the advancement of the Christian cause, shall we offer her the consolation of a God who suffers by proclaiming salvation for those who are innocently killed, regardless and independent of demands for the fulfilment of earthly justice? Would not that be akin to a repeated killing of her loved ones, but this time even more monstrous, because it takes place at an infinitely refined theoretical level, that is, where human suffering is being theologically codified, sublimated, and ultimately "reconciled" in the concept of the God who suffers, but without practical consequence for our lives?

Whoever wishes to bridge this manifest and uneasy absence of God in the experience of human suffering by its interpretive transference into God does not create intimacy of faith but actually multiplies the suffering in the world. On the other hand, if it does not want to succumb to the accusations of utmost apathy and indifference, what options are there for theology to speak with authority about the God who suffers in the face of such abominable horrors? If theology must (indeed, should it?) speak out from the bloody circles of mass murders and genocide, could it be done outside the casual numbness and absurdity of theological necromancy designed to assist our sense of being ultimately abandoned by God in the experience of violence and terror, in the attitude of rage and lancinating pain in which one does not know how or simply does not want to discover God in the act of a new, reconciliatory creation? Anyone who believes that these issues can be dealt with or endured in the unruffled equanimity of Christian soteriological discourse has not yet set foot into the darkness of negation and unrest beyond all religious self-evidence, beyond idolatry of certainty, and learned ignorance of our fundamental theological notions and assumptions; certainly he has not neared that inaccessible chasm of human crime and guilt that still holds the bones of slain mothers and fathers, sisters and brothers, daughters and sons ... through the darkness which groans with unrest that theology now besieges with an unbearable stench of forgetfulness and indifference as witness to its own impossibility of dealing with the dark side of God.

In an earlier text I acknowledged the impact of Moltmann's theology on my first attempts at contextualizating the theology of the cross.[9] In a section of the text—presumptively, rather than systemically—I proposed the article on Jesus's descent into hell of the Apostles' Creed as a prolegomenon to the contextual challenges of Christian theology in Bosnia and Herzegovina. Those first impulses arising from an early understanding of Moltmann's theology—as well as the concomitant artificiality and contextual affectation typical of the work of a young theologian—are still with me. On that occasion, however, I did not omit to mention that I owed the originality of that insight to Ivan Šarčević, OFM, at the time my professor of pastoral theology at the Franciscan Theology in Sarajevo. I still remember him vividly, standing in front of our class in his honest wrestling with that troubling article of faith in the most dramatic and intellectually engaging twists and turns.

Without desire to dwell any further on this seemingly irrelevant and personal vignette, I mention it only to recall my initial discomfort, even repulsion, with a theology that finds expression in the mystery of the abandoned Christ, in his suffering and agonizing death—a mystery for which I regularly had more intellectual forbearance than experiential audacity of faith. Theology of Good Friday, then and today, stands for me under the mark of that psychological ineptitude to seize faith out of the experience of a life pressed by an irresolvable burden of human suffering. I did not know what it meant for me to stand under the mark of unresolvable deficiency in my own faith, and with meager theological perspectives, perfectly consistent with borrowed certainties and designed to preserve the logical coherence of life under the assault of internal and external incoherencies. *Cur Deus Hommo* proved to be an unsatisfying interpretive framework which could no longer be coherently retained at an experiential level.

9. Šeperić, "Političnost k(o)ristoljublja."

Entoni Šeperić *Theological Discourse in the Vicious Circle of Apathy*

That is, in short, how I came across Moltmann's theology. *The Crucified God* was listed in the course literature, and it immediately struck a chord with me. In the abundance of first-rate but essentially disinterested theology as far as human suffering is concerned, Moltmann's personal experiences reasserted the priority of a historically based narrative—rather than abstract concepts of divinity—in theological reflection. His theology of the cross was in essence a radicalization of the *sola scriptura* principle through the contextual restatement and reinterpretation of Luther's axiom *crux sola nostra theologia* in the light of a concrete experience of human suffering. It was an alternative interpretive framework that I could easily connect not only with the rich Franciscan theological heritage, which shares that basically Augustinian impetus with its own innate nerve for the theological primacy of human experience (*haecceitas*), but also with my own postwar experience of personal disorientation and disturbance caused by unfathomable human pain and suffering.

The images and experiences of the *liminality* of our contextual situation—the impression of being caught up in between the regular concepts of time and space—had a deep impact on the theological reflection of my generation. True acknowledgements of contextual preconditions for our own theology in a postwar setting, as some of us believed, should have resulted in *kenotic* practices, and empty our discourse of inflated universalities which were so prominent in our school theology. The latter, however, proved to be a bad conjecture; the grave challenges of identity and difference in a postwar society shattered every serious attempt at subversive and creative voices towards a "post-Srebrenica" theology, rendering it completely marginal and socially irrelevant. An apology of ethno-national self-indulgence woven into a pseudo-Christian narrative of national deservedness and merit, a complete absence of self-criticism and second-rate reflection, blatant senselessness of simplification and theological travesty in service of the advancement of our national cause, full religious patronage in denial of our own part in crimes, and negation of mass murders and genocide have become the main preoccupation of local and regional theologies. Our theology is, therefore, in want of contrite Christian metaphors able to break through the "hermeneutical spiral" of corrosive national interpretive frameworks that feed on the conceptual substructures of a *Christus Victor* theology.

JESUS'S DESCENT INTO HELL

The article on Jesus's descent into hell in the Apostles' Creed is a constituent part of the Christian deposit of faith. The accompanying ornamental fancy and décor of mystery that found so many shiny expressions in the art of subsequent ages did not detract much from this well-attested fact. Historically speaking, however, it is one of the latest components of the Apostles' Creed. In fact, the baptismal creed of the church in Rome, which goes back to the second century, has no mention of Christ's descent into hell. It is not present in the Nicene Creed either. Furthermore, it is underrepresented in the church's liturgical tradition and plays no particular role even during Easter Triduum. While the doctrine of the Jesus's descent at first glance constitutes a completely marginal element in Christian teaching, the stretching of its conceptual potentialities resulted in layers of varying and at times conflicting historical interpretations.

It is difficult for me to speculate about the real reasons, but the doctrine of Jesus's descent is virtually absent from the works of contemporary systematic theology. Even when it does find a place in systemic theological reflection—and almost by default in cases when it cannot be simply dismissed or avoided, such as in the commentaries of the Apostles' Creed—it is so hastily wrapped in theological randomness, and indeed appears to be some alien appendage, rather than an essential part of Christian deposit of faith. In fact, as we shall see later, there is a double nervousness concerning this article of faith: one less innocent and associated with the typical crisis of the relevance of Christian theology and the content of its proclamation, and the other, in its consequences far more dangerous and less innocent, resonating with the prevailing culture of forgetfulness, especially the forgetfulness of victims and their suffering.

Contemporary Catholic theology is not rich in systematic theological reflection on this article of faith either. Hans Urs von Balthasar, however, is an exception to the rule. He offered an interpretation that—despite occasional awkwardness and obscurities that would have put even Origen to shame—bears significant impact on subsequent Catholic theology. His theological and prayerful wrestling with redemptive intricacies of the paschal mystery is most fully represented in his theological meditation—*Mysterium Paschale*. Yet to understand and appreciate the full breadth of his arguments, one must be acquainted with the rest of his massive theological undertaking and deduce general flows of argument from his highly aestheticized theological idiom. Because his theological project is not of first importance here, I will only sketch out his main argument with regards to the doctrine, which will suffice to illustrate my point.

One of Balthasar's leading theses is that Christ, in order to redeem humanity from punishment for sin, has to assume all the consequences of that sin. It would be simplest to say that his theology of Jesus's descent, and probably his theology in general, is in fact a heteronomous patchwork of insights woven into a strikingly coherent whole by means of highly aestheticized theological idiosyncrasy, which is in essence compatible with the classical penal substitution theory of the atonement. And it is exactly the model of penal substitution which is central to his theology and attracts the most attention from his critics, so much so that his whole theological edifice could be interpreted as starting from it as a hermeneutical key. Our intention here, however, is more modest; I want to press his model of penal substitution against the background of a reality marked by mass murder and genocide and uncover certain ideological elements pertaining to such theological "codification" of suffering.

Jesus's descent into hell is for Balthasar, who stands in line with the mainstream Catholic tradition, essentially descent into the abyss of the damned. Human death and damnation are punishments, or a price to be paid, due to the original and personal sins of mankind. In order to pay a perfect ransom for the sins of humanity, for every sin ever committed, Christ must suffer a complete and perfect punishment, a "super-punishment," so to say. This is in line with other well-known and historically attested penal substitution models. But what makes Balthasar's model so strikingly different and, indeed, novel—so much so that it probably should be regarded as unique in the history of theology—cannot be fully acknowledged without reference to the final consequences that such an insight triggers in his Christology, especially in his theology of the Trinity. In what follows I will try to dissect, to my best hermeneutical ability, what I find particularly striking in his model, and only point out a few particular issues that must remain open for further theological analysis.

As I have already hinted, Balthasar's theology of Jesus's descent is a very strong (probably the strongest) version of the penal substitutionary model. His account of the penal substitution, however, switches the soteriological priority away from the death of Jesus on the cross—Balthasar shows a general lack of aptitude and nerve for historicity—to the suffering of Christ in hell, or *Sheol*. This juxtaposition of the historical Jesus and his suffering on the cross with the suffering of Christ in hell are in no way incidental, but constitute a *differentia specifica* of his model of atonement. Threats to intrasystemic logical coherence force him to make increasingly odd theological inferences, which indeed sit uncomfortably with the rest of the Catholic tradition. Jesus's earthly suffering and his subsequent death on the cross are nothing compared to his suffering in Sheol, where he bears the full brunt of human sin, past and future alike. The brunt of human sin is so heavy that it cannot be simply borne by the human soul of Christ—because the utmost incommensurability of humanity and divinity, as well as the logical stringency of incarnational soterio-*logic* would not allow it—but by the divine person alone. And what makes it even more interesting, it is the divine person of the Son, which is not only stripped of any human quality, but also marked by a kenotic loss of all the privileges of divinity and, so to say, *ontologically* naked.

This divine suffering is then transferred into a trinitarian framework of thought and suffused with a large theo-drama that takes place between the Father, the Son, and the Holy Spirit.[10] Balthasar's trinitarian speculation, however, poses a serious challenge not only to the traditional teaching of the Catholic Church, but also to contemporary Catholic theology. It is no surprise that uncritically emphatic calls for his theological glorification often mix with those demanding the action of the Magisterium. Be it as it may, Balthasar's trinitarian logic is a serious incursion into traditional theological themes, since it locates creation and human sin in some sort of *distance* that exists in the perichoresis of the Father and the Son, and which is bridged by the Spirit functioning as a bond that maintains the unity. A more thorough study of the spiritual inheritance of Adrienne von Speyr, however, would probably offer more substantial answers to the main impulses in Balthasar's line of argumentation, rather than a comprehensive analysis of contemporary and classical Catholic theology.

In such a line of thought, every single element and every action on the side of the incarnate Son must also correspond—like a finely tuned instrument—to elements and movements in the dynamics of the immanent Trinity, so that the death of the Son, so to say, becomes a model of the *super-death* in the Trinity.[11] Of course, as soon as you allowed for the inner dictates of an intra-systemic logical coherence of a theological method to play the tune, then one inference calls for another, and very soon this *super-death* demands a sort of *super-kenosis* within the Trinity, allows for postulation of some *super-time* within the Trinity, etc. I am quite positive that Balthasar would not mind the allusion—to the contrary, I am sure that he would even have liked it!—but his grandiose ordering of the affairs of the world (along with the accompanying pathos that the word *grandeur* carries in arts) forms a masterly elaborate

---

10. Balthasar's theology of the Trinity is rather complex, and I will refrain from drawing comprehensive and final conclusions here. However, Mansini offers an interesting insight with a particular reference to the problem of God's immutability; see Mansini, "Balthasar and the Theodramatic Enrichment of the Trinity."

11. See Pitstick, *Light in Darkness*, 124–25.

and polished theological "round up" in conceptual arrangements of the Trinity, which is in fact perfectly akin to playing a Rachmaninov piano concerto, but without the usual constraints posed by the deficiencies of the instrument itself or arising from the lack of skill on the side of the player. And even if was never possible for Balthasar to achieve that completely, I am quite certain that he died aspiring to it.

If I am to draw, finally, any conclusions from Balthasar's interpretation of Jesus's descent into hell, I would prefer to insist on three matters of theological relevance. First, his penal substitutionary model of atonement, which in fact better resonates with the tradition of the Reformation[12] rather than with the Catholic one, is at best a theological *free-wheeling*, which dangerously infringes on and bounces off of the understanding of human freedom as we take it in the post-Enlightenment West. I find this point worth exploring. It is exactly this element—and especially his almost mechanical understanding of divine justice and mercy and the substitutionary penal model, in which the amount of divine punishment and suffering corresponds to every sin of humanity ever committed—that in fact renders the meaning and significance of human freedom, as well as human actions, as ultimately insignificant. Human suffering is perceived only as if an exponent of *balancing out* of suffering *internalized* in the inner mystery of God.

The confirmation that I might actually be right in this assumption is found in the fact that Balthasar, since he must offer a logical answer to this dilemma of finite freedom (*libertas creata, humana*) versus infinite freedom (*libertas increata, divina*), simply locates creation itself within the dynamics in the Trinity, to be precise, in the "distance" between the Father and the Son, where also human sins are "contained," and in fact neutralized, or appeased. Second, that "appeasement" in God—to make it even more strange—is the cause of the ever increasing and mutual enrichment between the Father and the Son, so that Balthasar does not refrain from speaking of God's increasing *perfection* in love

---

12. Ibid., 333.

after incarnation, postulating even some sort of *economic* event in God's eternal life.[13] It goes without saying that much of this poses serious hermeneutical trouble not only for our historicized, post-Enlightenment way of thinking, but also for the simplest fact of dealing with human suffering. It would be as if you would have approached—if I dare put it like that—a child with a lollipop and a smiling face who is about to be brutally killed, because, ultimately, the act of the brutal killing will somehow *enrich* the bond of love between the Father and the Son; but this, too, I must leave for another occasion.

And, third, Balthasar's theology as a whole, and particularly his theology of Jesus's descent, actually runs the risk of a particularly devious theological determinism, which is not discernible at first glance, because it is in essence identical to that already enculturated social epiphenomenon, i.e., the neglect of victims and low regard for the underdogs of history. Balthasar's theology, and there is a certain irony attached to it, is probably the best existing illustration of what it ultimately means theologically to perceive human creation and salvation not as a *trans*historical redemption *of* the world but as an *a*historical—and, if I may add, aesthetical—rescue *from* the world, which is so characteristic of the *Communio* school of thought.[14] Let us reiterate, salvation is a universal theme, the theme of humanity, or it is no theme at all; yet, does it make a world of difference to someone who has been badly treated, let alone brutally tortured and killed? Unless we hold on firmly to both parts of this truth, we are not preserving something absolutely central to Christianity, and it is exactly that which Balthasar, I honestly believe, did not find worth preserving.

---

13. Cf. Balthasar, *Last Act*, 513.

14. I do not have enough space nor time to further extend and elaborate my point, but it remains extremely unclear why—and this would be, indeed, a point worth exploring—the most ardent criticism of Balthasar's theology comes from theologians who are either very close to *Communio*, or simply share the same theological views of the group. Is this to be attributed to simple human envy, or is it, indeed, telling of a deeper and theologically more fundamental breach?

A THING IS A THING, AND NOT WHAT IS SAID (OF THAT THING)

Even this all too brief survey of Balthasar's theology of Jesus's descent has shown that there are indeed certain points, and more than just points, in his thought which will probably continue to provoke theological reaction. And it is rightly so. But I want to say a little more at this stage about one level of reactions to Balthasar's theology in particular. It is a level at which critics tend to focus on the problem of the formal and substantial compatibility of his theology with mainstream Catholic doctrine, ranging from unreserved, not to say emphatic, endorsements to the most radical and ardent opposition, which go so far as to evoke claims of heresy.

It is not my intention to give a detailed account of the contemporary Balthasarian scholarship, nor do I want to pretend that I am particularly familiar with all the major currents of interpretation. It is a task that would have probably made me feel somewhat like a man in his lumberjack shoes trying to imitate a ballet dancer performing an *arabesque*. What I will do, instead, is to point to a particularly interesting episode in the reception of his work, which will, I believe, not only help me to better emphasize my own points of disagreement with Balthasar's theology of Jesus's descent, but also point to an ideological element in the contemporary theological discourse.

The critique of Balthasar's theology of Jesus's descent came into strident expression in the work of American scholar Alyssa L. Pitstick.[15] The controversy surrounding her critical reading of Balthasar first started as a benign exchange of theological opinions, soon to be blown out of proportion, and even resulting in the deployment of heavy theological artillery.[16] The fact that it initially took place at the site of the journal *First Things*, which many consider to be among the most influential conservative American journals of religious affairs and public life, certainly gave a certain tinge to the prevailing tone of the dispute. Who would have

15. Pitstick, *Light in the Darkness*.
16. See *First Things* 168 (2006), and subsequent issues.

thought that such a marginal *quaestio disputata*, such as a theological analysis of the article of Jesus's descent into hell, could attract so much attention and cause such a heated exchange of opinions? Moreover, the atmosphere that dominated the discussion gave the impression that not only a simple truth of faith, but essentially the destiny of Christianity had been put to the test.

The fact that Pitstick's criticism was aimed at the questioning of the orthodoxy of one of the pivots of contemporary Catholic theology soon assumed precedence over the content of her arguments. I must admit that at first I sympathized with Pitstick, who has truly been exposed to rather heavy, and somewhat excessive criticism. To attack Balthasar—the giant of contemporary Catholic theology and, if he had lived for another day, probably the Curia cardinal—simply screamed for more than a solid argument. But her arguments were solid. In fact, she was not denying that Balthasar was indeed a great theologian, but that his theology simply was not Catholic, at least if we are to judge from his professedly unorthodox positions with regards to Jesus's descent, and from a great deal of other things, too. And yes, like a great number of reversed iconoclasts, she was to some extent right; she uncovered what it means to inquire about some of the supposed "fixed points" in contemporary Balthasarian scholarship, which may perhaps have been allowed to remain in place by fear of being considered unscholarly if one challenges it. Now, let us cursorily turn to her argument.

Pitstick's thesis, if taken at the simplest level, claims that Balthasar's theology of Jesus's descent is not only at odds with, but seriously *distorts* the Catholic doctrine. Due to the positions developed in his treatment of Jesus's descent, which also affected his whole theology, Balthasar, in her opinion, makes a series of grave concessions with the Catholic doctrine, including that of the Trinity, Christology, and even Mariology. It was already noted that Balthasar's theological freewheeling manner does not sit comfortably with the Catholic tradition. Indeed, her thesis, *prima facie*, appears to be a completely logical and intellectually very honest inference with which we can, indeed, agree or disagree, but Pitstick simply does not allow less than that the content of the doctrine in question be as strong as concrete. Pitstick wants us to believe that the article of Jesus's descent relates to fully rounded and substantially harmonized doctrinal content, rather than to a dogmatic kaleidoscope containing only loose, colored beads and pebbles of extremely vague and imperfect allusions, which can, indeed, form rather colorful and interesting patterns when rotated around a theological axis. But what *is*—and is there at all—a coherent doctrine about Jesus's descent into hell?

Pitstick not only believes that there is, but applies all her powers and skill—which are, not to sound malicious, indeed first-rate and outstanding—to meticulously dissect consecutive layers of historical, liturgical, doctrinal, and many other materials, and show in all its brilliance that the traditional doctrine of descent does not only involve Jesus's descent *ad inferos*, or into the "limbo of the fathers" but that this descent is in fact—and what she regards to be of utmost theological importance—*glorious*. Furthermore, it seems very important for her to underline that it is a descent of the divine person of the Son by means of his human soul, and it does not involve suffering, which is radically different from what Balthasar says. Christ's redemptive action, therefore, is not one focused on the amount of suffering, but on the *merit* of the suffering Christ. To document and better illustrate her position, Pitstick extensively quotes Scripture, the early Christian documents, traditional art, various liturgical texts—culminating in the teaching of the *Doctor Communis*—and a list of various church statements.

It is not my intention to delve into the fine intricacies of doctrinal criticism, but if we are to do justice to Pitstick's attempt, rather than splitting hairs on the word meanings, then she was probably right in pointing out that something was amiss in Balthasar's theology. To that I am giving my full consent. Yet what seems particularly disturbing in Pitstick's treatment of Balthasar's theology is not so much the fact that she uses the argument from tradition to press Balthasar on issues that he was altogether aware of but simply *ignored*, as it is the way in which she employs the argument to serve a particular purpose in such a totalizing sway, which may indeed force us to make precise interpretative judgements, but which essentially remains a fine example of the alienation of contemporary academic theology from the core issues that it purportedly conveys; in other words, the meaning is completely lost in the passive set of formal utterances. But let us first clarify the matter. Pitstick was chosen solely for the purpose of illustration; what I intended to say, however, aims at a more fundamental level and calls for our full engagement with a range of issues—certainly not only theological—that pertain to what it means to practice theology in the context of Srebrenica, of mass murders and genocide, and resist that cautious minimalism that threatens here as elsewhere to reduce scholarship to mere embattled silence, or yet to another fight over semantics.

GETTING HELL OUT OF HERE

If we are to draw any conclusions from Balthasar's theology, as well as from some of its most recent criticism, it certainly be to remind us how difficult it is to salvage a piece of candy from the piñata god of our doctrinal propositions, which is constantly being struck by the appalling horrors of the world. I am absolutely certain that Balthasar was fully aware of this drama, too, and that he conceived of this drama—only to evoke the title of his massive theological undertaking—as the drama of God, which is the fact at the heart of his theology. Whoever claims otherwise really misses the point of his theology. It is another issue, however, whether his "novel perspective" cut against the grain of preceding Catholic tradition and theology by pushing the limits of normative dogmatic language. I leave this issue to those better equipped, though I reserve the right to provide some final intimations regarding Balthasar's theology, even at the cost of complete misreading.

To pay attention to the underlying structure of Balthasar's thought is not simply a matter of recognizing the implicit theological problems and dubious catches, and drawing out their implications for systematic theology. Something much deeper, and in my view dangerously *ideological*, exists at the heart of Balthasar's theology, which leaves no room for the Pauline view of the cross of the Messiah, and for the consequent critique of all human pride and systems. Of course, we can go on debating what precisely that ideological content was, and I am sure it would happily take an entire book to explain, but I will take the risk of suggesting that the only discernible thing from Balthasar's theology is that totalizing "subjectivity" of divine consciousness, which is definitely not a subject, let alone human. His theology is, therefore, so irreparably and, perhaps, intentionally totalitarian, that it can be almost perfectly paralleled with what Hegel did in philosophy.

It is quite obvious that ever since the publication of Lindbeck's seminal work *The Nature of Doctrine*, it has become increasingly difficult to maintain a cognitive-propositional approach to Christian doctrine in the privatistic setting of contemporary Western thought with its high regard for the incommensurable truth of each and every individual. We may express serious reservations about his conclusions, or even strongly disapprove of them, but it is glaringly obvious that propositional discourse can no longer dispense with a threefold set of major concerns: historical, exegetical, and of contemporary relevance. Each of these concerns, none of which are free of implicit challenges or concomitant dangers, opens up a whole range of theologically relevant issues that cannot be discarded without serious consequences. Christian orthodoxy, however, cannot be equated with a psychological situation of mere "structural uncertainties" resulting from the gradual destabilization of Christian identity in the context of social pluralism.

We can probably agree that Christian confessional forms and credal formulae are not the mere controlling paradigms of communal conceptual potentialities, but that they may also function as regulative frameworks of individual conduct. This seems to be an obvious fact, and in some strands of Christianity quite more so than in others. If one of the core functions of a doctrine, then, is to define communities of discourse by means of effective social cohesion which *also* requires fixing the boundaries—and not only through delimitation of what must be placed within, but still more so through defining what must be omitted or left outside—is it not, then, perfectly legitimate to ask about the extent to which changes of interpretive nuances in doctrinal formulations reflect actual changes in the sociopolitical, mental, and/or emotional situation of their generating community? What shifts or changes, if any, are we able to identify in our communal hermeneutical framework with regards to the article of Jesus's descent into hell? It is here that we lack an answer from Pitstick, but in all honesty we must concede that it would not have been fair to expect it, due to the simple fact that it did not pertain to the main subject of her research.

What I wanted to say with this somewhat lingering argumentation, however, is that the predominance and insistence on the formal criteria of orthodoxy to the detriment of the content of a normative conceptual claim within a community of discourse may *also* be telling of a shift or change in its experiential framework. Is not our inability to demand engagement with a view (or range of views) of reality already domesticated and immunized by a particular propositional language or conceptual framework shaped by already exhausted patterns of worship, adoration, and prayer, and thus made completely irrelevant and non-subversive, a sufficient witness to such a change? I strongly believe that there is a connection between this particular inability and formal insistence on ideological soundness, not to say purity, of our confessional forms that not only abstracts our faith from its proper theological content, but also reveals a crucial change in our social locations. In other words, if all means of social demarcation associated with the Christian experience have a clear doctrinal component, then it is perfectly acceptable to suggest that it outlines a new form of social demarcation in Christian communal experience. What is, theologically speaking, a social locus of the Christian community of discourse which perceives the pathos of God as the cause of Christ's suffering on our behalf, even unto the depths of human existence, *solely* in the images and language of triumph and glory? In fact, willful ignorance or refusal to be aware of the repugnant factuality of mass murder and genocide are constitutive for all theological attempts at calming and taming the embarrassing return-questions that bounce back through the air of our prevailing cultural amnesia.[17]

While locating our discussion within our own culture, and if our position is thus to be further relativized, I cannot refrain from posing a rather naïve question. Can this iconographic motif of the glorious Christ who redeems Adam, Eve, and all of the patriarchs and righteous ones, really be set against the uneasiness and misery of the world, and disperse the stink of the "atmospheric Nietzsche" (Metz) that has permeated our deleterious Western culture, but without the slightest hint or even reminiscence of the theodicy question? I do not think so. And I will immediately embark on a course of arguing as strongly as I can that it is by no means a marginal question, or a simple side effect of theological freewheeling gone wrong. Instead, I argue, it is a symptom of a radical shift in the social locus of Christianity and Christian theology in Europe and America in particular. This shift is marked by a complete and almost irretrievable slippage into brutal neglect of victims and their suffering, slippage to which theology—such as that of Balthasar—lends its highly mythicized and aestheticized language to further blur the ever thinner mark of wasted metaphysical responsibility inscribed on the faces of those who suffer.

If this question is not important for theology, then, which one is? But whichever way we look at it, this question is pressing and unavoidable, and its importance is further accentuated within a context where our inflated certainties and logomachy are able to create far more human misery than what is usually permitted in open discussion.

The article on Jesus's descent into hell is not, indeed, some marginal conceptualization of Christian faith. It discloses one particularly disturbing part of the paschal mystery, that is, Jesus's actual experience of *going through* his physical death and agony and the meaning it conveys to us. To approach this mystery solely on the basis of a particular "nervousness" of the soteriological argument—which pertains to the propositional language of the church's dogmatic statements, as well as to certain strands of

17. Cf. Metz, *Memoria passionis*.

systematic theology—is to dangerously minimize that conspicuous and palpable and, I strongly believe, intentional *powerlessness* of the original Christian witness to express in words the exact content of Jesus's death, apart from images and language already contained and mirrored in their understanding of Jesus's meritorious—and, indeed, *triumphant*—deeds. Need I particularly emphasize the fact that it was essentially an *ex post* inference of those who had found new faith in Jesus, but only after initially succumbing to the brutal factuality of his agonizing death and dying? In a special way, perhaps, the Apostles' Creed article on Jesus's descent might also preserve for us an often so brutally misappropriated and particularly despised religious awareness, namely that God's revelation is neither constituted nor conveyed, or at least not exclusively so, by means of his explicit word or proclamation, but still more by God's silence or complete absence of utterance.

Unless we have already given way to negative theology, or even slipped into the purely mythicized thought and language conducive to our growing cultural amnesia, then we must come to grips with that particular soteriological ardency of our propositional theological discourse and language, which has become so prevalent not only in our intellectual and scholarly debates, but also in our church practice and public witness. It comes as no surprise, then, that this ardency lends heat to discussions on socially delimiting functions of the doctrine in its desire to preserve the integrity and soundness of Christian belief under the full assault of outward and, to be sure, inner inconsistencies. Yet, can this integrity be preserved solely on the grounds of theological "objectivization" of a language marked by a conceptual transferral, or even complete removal, of all subversive emphasis from the issue of real effects and consequences of Christ's redemptive work, and sociopolitical wherewithal, to the issue of individual salvation, which is so well domesticated and integral to our soteriologically egotistical Western civilization? In other words, can it convey and communicate meanings other than that already settled and pacified in our bourgeois consciousness of individual or collective assessments of Christian salvation, but without the slightest hint of disturbance caused by the factuality of mass murders and genocide? It is a thing to ponder.

This is exactly where we ought to be open to considering the value and purpose of being a theologian, if not a Christian, too. Is there any purpose—and, more importantly, what are the prospects—for a theology that does not want to be playfully satisfied with the highly formalized language of orthodoxy, which does not succumb to the status of a morally indifferent bystander of human crime and genocide, and does not vacillate between the daydream of its own hermeneutical innocence and self-delusions of its own social importance or relevance? If theology is indeed a disciplined reflection on faith and thus also on God's revelation, and if it still seeks to serve the church by accurately establishing the content of both faith and revelation by critical assessment of its rich tradition, our local and regional theologies must, then, reassess their own stands with regards to their purported hermeneutical innocence and grave misconduct before, during the war, and in the postwar period.

On the other hand, if there is still anything left from the original authenticity of the Christian proclamation, how can we feed our all too human anguish with feelings of moral superiority of those who are, perhaps, not personally inclined to commit, yet perfectly approving of that crime? If we as theologians are no more ready to stand in opposition to the crimes of mass murder and genocide in complacent silence and in the crime of gross disregard for victims, then we must also renounce in contrition and counter all the social and political benefits that may have been brought about by religion's sponsorship of the structural sin of silence and forgetfulness of victims—indeed, of *all* victims, not simply ours or theirs. But is this still possible? And what else is to be done with an awareness of that almost monstrous semblance of self-righteousness in our virtually untouched and unharmed moral perspectives, while in quiescence we observe the desolating sacrilege in our holy places? Are we not like the whitewashed tombs, on the outside decorated with a blissful mimicry of learned ignorance and all sorts of cynicism but on the inside with a pestilent stench of silence and willful ignorance of the scattered bones of victims that are still crying out to us? To what exactly do we owe the patience of those who, due to the failures and shortcomings of earthly justice, still have to endure the faces of those who were their former torturers, of those who burnt their homes, of those who murdered their loved ones, and of those who have destroyed their entire lives, burdening them with the memories of something that can never be forgotten? Are those our faces as well?

If theology is, indeed, a disciplined reflection on faith and revelation, and if the act of faith actually precedes any faith and theology, than this expressionless stolidity of contemporary theological discourse for the orgy of mass murders and genocide may as well be a sign of an essential deficiency in contemporary Christian faith. Moreover, it seems entirely possible—even certain—that this "shortcoming" of our faith and theology protrudes out of an obvious surplus of the axiomatic and generalized awareness against the absurdity of human suffering, which is an indication of a deeper and unremitting tendency in contemporary Christian theology. To this tendency of theology—which finds it extremely difficult to abandon its own ideological inscribing "into" human history—and concomitant understanding of human historicity itself, which is marked by the lack of memory of victims and their suffering, Metz juxtaposes the praxis of "productive noncontemporaneity"[18] of dangerous memory, or *memoria passionis*. Theology that is aware of such a memory cannot put off or ignore all disturbing questions arising from the absurdity of human suffering in history by way of myth, in which these questions are always constitutively blasé, veiled, and ultimately silenced in full forgetfulness of their real source and meaning, and certainly not in remembrance of those who suffered. And it is perhaps because of that reason that one of the most reliable ways to get an insight into the constituent weakness of a society is through careful exposition of what that society has excluded from its own discourse.

---

18. Cf. Metz, "Productive Noncontemporaneity."

CONCLUSION

What the early Christian tradition perceived in Jesus's descent into hell, as Pitstick rightly observed, was surely the manifestation of his victory over death and the revelation of the first fruits of redemption. Yet we ought to rediscover its true meaning beyond the concomitant pathos and ornament of triumphalism with which the subsequent theological reasoning so happily veiled its own ignorance of victims and the underdogs of history. Neutrality is impossible; the observer effect simply does not apply in circumstances where theology faces a hermeneutical framework within which such ideological endowments of theology over ethno-nationalism, as well as its complicity in the evils committed, can neither be dismissed nor ignored. To what extent the Christian hermeneutics of history has contributed to the horrific crimes and genocide that marked my generation will long remain open to critical theological research. Despite the blissful hindsight of memory and its ready-made excuses—which always spring from practical, rather than theoretical lack of interest in *humanum*—our regional theologies are affected by the deep crisis of relevance, as well as a lack of credibility with regards to their hermeneutic innocence. Our theology is stuck in a dense fog of complacent habit and insensitivity towards the factuality of terrible mass murders and genocide within our carefully cultivated culture of forgetting, which has already become akin to a life project for so many of us.[19] A daunting task is still ahead of us.

Our theology is indeed in want of contrite theological metaphors. It is far easier, not to say less disturbing, to feign theologically informed rationalizations, than to be drawn out of the devil's circle of complacent and tacit ignorance of our ghetto mentality and its masquerade of nonnegotiables. Though a fuller presentation of the gravity of our particular *theo-political* situation would have required more contextual explication and analysis, it was my hope, however, that by expounding upon our particular case we

---

19. For the most recent attempt at critical and contextual consideration of religion in our context, see Sremac et al., *Opasna sjećanja*.

will be able to hint at some problems that emerge from a wider discussion on religion and politics in our world, and point to a possible contextual contribution of our local theology to a world church. I am painfully aware that the impediments of my own theological perspective—which deliberately rejects any theological normativity uninformed by the factuality of mass murder and genocide—prevent me from neutral estimates of theologically pertinent issues, which will have to remain, unfortunately, under the mark of incompleteness, but which will also, I hope, better disclose its biographical undertone.

BIBLIOGRAPHY

Balthasar, Hans Urs von. *The Last Act*. Vol. 5 of *Theo-Drama: Theological Dramatic Theory*. Translated by Graham Harrison. San Francisco: Ignatius, 1998.

———. *Mysterium Paschale: The Mystery of Easter*. Translated by Aidan Nichols. Edinburgh: T. & T. Clark, 1990.

Lindbeck, George A. *The Nature of Doctrine: Religion and Theology in a Postliberal Age*. 1st ed. Philadelphia: Westminster, 1984.

Mansini, Guy. "Balthasar and the Theodramatic Enrichment of the Trinity." *Thomist* 64 (2000) 499–519.

Metz, Johannes Baptist. *Memoria Passionis: Ein provozierendes Gedächtnis in pluralistischer Gesellschaft*. Freiburg im Breisgau: Herder, 2006.

———. "Productive Noncontemporaneity." In *Observations on "The Spiritual Situation of the Age": Contemporary German Perspectives*, edited by Jürgen Habermas, translated by Andrew Buchwalter, 169–77. Cambridge: MIT, 1984.

Moltmann, Jürgen. *The Crucified God: The Cross of Christ as Foundation and Criticism of Christian Theology*. Translated by R. A. Wilson and John Bowden. Minneapolis: Fortress, 1993.

Pitstick, Alyssa Lyra. *Light in Darkness: Hans Urs von Balthasar and the Catholic Doctrine of Christ's Descent into Hell*. Grand Rapids: Eerdmans, 2007.

Pitstick, Alyssa Lyra, and Edward T. Oakes. "Balthasar, Hell, and Heresy: An Exchange." *First Things* 168 (2006). http://www.firstthings.com/article/2006/12/balthasar-hell-and-heresy-an-exchange.

———. "More on Balthasar, Hell, and Heresy." *First Things* 169 (2007). http://www.firstthings.com/article/2007/01/003-more-on-balthasar-hell-and-heresy.

Ruether, Rosemary Radford. *To Change the World: Christology and Cultural Criticism*. New York: Crossroad, 1981.

Šeperić, Entoni. "Političnost k(o)ristoljublja." In *Bog pred križem: Zbornik u čast Jürgena Moltmanna*, edited by Zoran Grozdanov, 99–131. Rijeka: Ex libris, 2007.

Sremac, Srđan, et al., eds. *Opasna sjećanja i pomirenje: Kontekstualna promišljanja o religiji u postkonfliktnom društvu*. Rijeka: Ex libris, 2011.

5

The Pretense Veil of Christian Vulgarism

Ethno-religious Wraith in Contemporary Secular Society

—Branko Sekulić

"You'll see the face of the traitor. But don't get taken in by appearances: a traitor's face can take on a look of great righteousness."[1]

—Danilo Kiš, *Tomb for Boris Davidovich*

---

1. Kiš, *Tomb for Boris Davidovich*, 9.

BOASTFUL *DEPOSITUM FIDEI* OF RELIGIONISM

POLITICAL RELIGION IS A vulgarized veil that is put over the face of genuine religiosity by certain church groups in an effort to show the strength of universality in the context of Christian mission, within an extremely narrow-minded framework of mere politicking, and for the sole interest of particular social interest groups. Religion thus turns into *religionism*, i.e., it reverses into its opposite, becoming a perverse system of belief which is, despite its insistence on the divine qualities of faith, actually devoid of any divine passion. These aberrations manifest themselves primarily through the enthronement of the most primitive form of confessional worship: the worship and idealization of the regime. This kind of engaged service then breaks the spirit of Christian fellowship, thus causing wounds on the body of the general appeal to the gospel while threatening the humanist harmony of particular social surroundings.

This, so to speak, energetic plug hinders the original Christian teaching while dosing it in limited batches, primarily through the filters of regional initiatives of certain individuals, and creates a sort of spiritual vacuum in the life of a nation and its confession, inevitably affecting the entire system of social paradigms that sustain a society. In other words, this lockdown prevents smooth circulation of progressive thoughts and lifestyles, thus creating a religious clot with serious existential repercussions, expressed through a narrowed-minded image of political worship turning into an atrocious precedent in a complex set of daily trends and developments of a given state and its citizens.

> People are also more keenly and painfully aware that a large part of the church is in one way or another linked to those who wield economic and political power in today's world. This applies to its position in the opulent and oppressive countries as well as in the poor countries, as in Latin America, where it is tied to the exploiting classes.[2]

---

2. Gutiérrez, *Theology of Liberation*, 40.

The political religion, therefore, as an official *modus operandi* of certain church elites, with their conceited politicized approach, which is entirely disconnected from any essential grounding in the heritage of faith (*depositum fidei*), becomes a rapacious intruder into the Christian value system, threatening not only the work of Christ but also the secular views of the society, creating in this way vehement animosity between the true moral standpoints and transient ideological content. This disharmonic process disguises the enormous force of pent-up frustrations enshrouding an unquenchable desire for clear sublimation of commendable human aspirations, carried by the possibility of concrete social definition where faith would be devoid of any depreciative features of *religionism*, and the society would become free of all disheartening *politicking*.

It is exactly this area of contention that will be taken as the departure point for our engagement if we are to avoid becoming the eternal prisoners of the imposed aberrant rules. The society, through the authentic faith of the church, can enrich our life with the true meaning of its own existence, and the faith of the church should be guided by the constructive criticism of everyday social processes and events, so as to make both of them a fulfillment rather than a degradation in the life of an individual, who is a fundamental sample serving as the building block for both the civil system of humanistic pledge, as well as the cornerstone of Christian dialogue. An individual encompasses the whole range of theological and civil efforts, and only the social reflection of the relationship between theological and civil dimensions represents the possibility of success of a certain civilization process. For this reason, our urgent task, primarily as human beings, and then also as professionals in the humanities, is to establish a diagnosis for the ongoing social events, i.e., to take off the pseudo-religious disguises while breaking quasi-political and self-serving circles concerned only with their own interests.

POLITICAL RELIGION: THE HISTORY OF THE DISEASE AND AN ETHNO-RELIGIOUS DIAGNOSIS

The political religion at its historical level suffers from a twofold lack of understanding. At the existential level, this is manifested in two forms of acute forgetfulness—the one towards the God of its own calling, and the other towards our neighbor as the prime recipient of theological proclamation. Both of the aforementioned settings clearly point to the potential danger of disintegrating the entire Christian worldview in a certain area in which the regime worshiping is maintained. It follows then that individual interests are restating firmly entrenched ethical norms and shaping them authoritatively through the undisputed power of the institutions. And in the case with the church and the state, whereby the entire value system of a society is warped, which consequently results in a considerable disorientation of citizens,

> Political idolatry and political alienation arise when the representatives go over the heads of those whom they are meant to represent, and when the people bows to its own rulers.[3]

Namely, a large part of the population, often guided blindly by the influence of socially prominent persons—in this context by the respective church and state dignitaries—mainly remain in the shadow of their own rash accommodation to the new situation and their concomitant non-critical thinking. They are becoming mere marionettes in a system of completely privatized intentions. This situation breeds a major set of misconceptions, gaining socially normative features that are more typical of obsolete feudal relations than of the contemporary democratic process. However, this economic-dependence structure of coexistence rests upon the centuries-old petrified symbols of power. They are successfully sublimating the fears of the masses through the ideological propaganda of politicking groups to the extent that any kind of

---

3. Moltmann, *Crucified God*, 328.

endangerment of this relationship often ends with the most aggressive reactions by this morally diseased and corrupt system.

That being said, we are coming to the essence of these politically colored relations. It becomes obvious that with the unflinching perseverance for the personal benefit of the regime and its undisputedly loyal minions, the situation results in a general deviation of a given social system. This inevitably leads to the erosion of the religious belief system, and the inability of a complete civil striving for the realization of human rights. Hence, this disrupted but potentially sweeping civilizational progress is thwarted through usurpation of public space by certain interest groups, hiding behind unstoppable axioms of political worship that are hard to overturn. With their own greedy and self-seeking ways of repressing the original demands of Christian teachings and democratic postulates, they have created a detiorated the body of religious and social expressions.

A caricature of religion is thus created, manifesting itself through two already mentioned views of acute forgetfulness—towards the God of its own calling and toward our neighbors (as the prime recipients of theological proclamation), distorting the image of the nature of Christ's work and the purpose of his selfless sacrifice to the world and human beings (Phil 2:7). This compliance of certain church structures with a regime that represses the laws of their own service for its own interests, thus indirectly creating the gaps in the memory of God's pledge of Covenant, tries to substitute those gaps in *the reservoir of holy memories* by way of their own private egoistic interpretations. The system based on forgetfulness is ultimately shaped in this way, making the political religion of a certain context a unique confessional construct, manifesting itself at the existential level of society as the ultimate expression of religious observance.

This makes the political worship the quintessential expression of faith or confession in the life of a nation, whose members overwhelmingly serve their duty in their unwitting obedience, guarding the grave of the aforementioned privatized truths, while identifying themselves with the imposed system as the only possible form of their own existence. Precisely this risky delusion *is* the hermeneutical circle of the aberration within which this entire system of pretense is being played out, whereby certain factions of religious communities try to proclaim themselves gods ruling over an area—of course, at the expense of their underlying values that they are now trying to rewrite by giving them some entirely different meanings.

> Holy Scripture is the unique text that the political religion most manipulates with. It mostly rejects any reference to the text (the Gospel), and if it uses it, it takes it in bits and pieces and partially, disregarding its wholeness, or in a fundamentalist manner in order to justify its daily political interest of the mobilization of the oppressed people.[4]

Our history abounds with cases when the church appeared to be no more than a political party with carefully honed intentions, rather than a socially constructive force, entirely stripped of any political interests, which builds the spiritual tissue of a concrete nation and serves the sole purpose of civil harmonization and dialogue. The church as the mother institution of Christian community, with its thousand-year-old confessional tradition, surely has the strength to support contemporary civil society in its attempts at substantial change in order to provide all humanistic security for the normal growth and development of a population in a certain area under the aegis of capacities provided by the clear secular worldviews and constructive religious tolerance. However, at least in our context (the Balkans), both members of various confessional affiliations and nonbelievers alike have more often been stakeholders in ploys of religious politicking than participants in concrete civilization coalescence in which various ethical views of human efforts would be accepted as enrichments rather than ideological threats to each other.

It is exactly at this point that the political religion, the subject of this discussion, holds one of the crucial places in the

---

4. Šarčević, "Politička religija," 19.

above-mentioned social division, indirectly becoming the object of a repugnant spiritual divergence. For, by accommodating its own essence to the shallow and raw populist urges, the political religion has built a limited viewpoint of narrow and confined ethnic features, leaving very little room for humanistic values. This, of course, makes it incapable for any serious appreciation within the frameworks of its own calling or secular moral incentives. This breeds ethno-religionism in the full force of noncomprehension of its own essence which has strictly Christian roots. This can be best observed in relationship towards the God of its own faith as well as in relations with fellow human beings, as direct objects of Christ's work of salvation.

ONE FLEW OVER THE ETHNO-RELIGIOUS NEST

Ethno-religionism as a concept of political-religious provenance is, I would say, a cardinal facet of confessional desertion and perpetual treason, entrenched in the incessant denial of Jesus's life and martyrdom, for the purpose of satisfying superficial interests and worldly needs. This latent move of turning one's back on the God of one's own faith, whilst his name is on the lips of those same questionable politicking church circles, has brought about a whole new world of blind, spiritual, poltroon, and pro-regime followers. I call it ethno-religious spiritualism in its twisted purport of the spiritual departure from Christ's example.

> Is not their misunderstanding on the same level as the misunderstanding of him by the Pharisees? Did not even his own disciples misunderstand him, as is shown by their flight from the cross?[5]

I would say they did, as I would also point out that exactly this New Testament example of judgment and escape contains a serious pre-image of the above-mentioned ethno-religious approach, clearly defined within the political religious pattern; as Ratzinger would put it, they are *pathological forms* of the Christian

---

5. Moltmann, *Crucified God*, 137.

teachings.⁶ The prototype of the governing ambition of some religious groups (the Pharisees) unequivocally stems from it, as well as the archetype of mute adherence of the people (the disciples) to the regime of the politically stronger factor. We should in no way and certainly in no respect give the contours of providence to this denial of the eternity of the faith which is often executed by certain religious institutions in the name of preservation of tradition.

> It is possible to think oneself sincerely religious and not be at all religious at heart; it is even possible to consider oneself a "traditionalist" without having the least notion of the real traditional spirit; and this is one more symptom of the mental confusion of our time.⁷

Tradition, therefore, is necessary and useful, but only when it opens up the possibility for the members of its society to question the institutional church within the current time period, and when it also acts constructively and self-critically. For, if *the truth* was one and indisputable, then the Earth would probably still be a flat panel. However, and unfortunately, in our case the situation appears to be exactly like creating a dangerous disguise woven from the delusions of political worship, which holds the concrete confession of faith of a certain social context in a disadvantaged position of carefully chosen and greedily censored truths. To be more precise, some church groups use this to stunt the growth of faith in strictly controlled municipal religious laboratories, using it as a metaphysical yeast for the artificial pumping up the politically colored myths. In this way, they are intimidating the nations of a certain area, such as the Western Balkans, where people are kept in constant fear of all possible changes. For that reason, they are assured that behind the horizon there is nothing but bare nothingness.

With these kinds of manipulations, the inhabitants of this area, metaphorically speaking, are entrapped within the *Pharisaical pre-image* of limiting religious interpretations. This image will

---

6. See Ratzinger, *Salt of the Earth*, 129–54.
7. Guénon, *Crisis of the Modern World*, 64.

hardly ever be characterized by the understanding of the emerging circumstances. On the contrary, it will rather adopt an attitude of primitive encroachment of raw urges, adorning them with religious features, for "it is obvious that religion has become an important resource for state politics, and state politics an important factor for the affirmation of religion."[8] This is then an overt, almost textbook pattern of how political religion, by means of its own ethno-religious derivative, assaults the postulates of its own mission and the society within which it exists. At a purely social level, this change is easily noticed, as it is publically manifested through specific quasi-folklore gatherings, mainly defined by chauvinist customs and supported by the one-sided or exclusivistic forms of Christianity. This "embedding of religious identity into the foundation of national identity and development of mass (secular) nationalism"[9] is a considerable sore spot for any society with democratic aspirations. For, instead of the dynamic of the faith, a religious passivity is being imposed on it, which slowly but surely corrodes the normal development of humanistic aspirations throughout the entire society.

This means, primarily, that the petrified principles of private mythologies, which in the shape of the *holy truths* are being served to the wider population in their everyday circumstances are presupposing the postulates of the true faith to the fullness of the freedom of Christian confessional and irrefutably humanistic testimony. In this way, a supple fellowship is formed which then often, when necessary, transforms itself in problematic communities of a militant features, dangerously immersed in the individual pseudo-patriotic service which is characterized by "politics of hypertrophied wishes, irresponsible promises, incoherent relation towards past, politics of illusory reconciliation of unbearable opposites and politics of unscrupulous manipulation with history, facts and ultimately with the people."[10] In short, it is characterized by ethno-religious spiritualism in the strategic service of creating

---

8. Vrcan, "Religija i politika," §III.
9. Roksandić, "Religious Tolerance and Division in the Krajina," 75.
10. Buden, *Barikade* 2, 86.

golden calves, beyond any humanity, yet carefully grounded in the discriminatory and politicized worshiping which gives birth to *the beast from the abyss*,[11] an ethno-religious wraith of political theology in a secular society.

This kind of abomination is primarily reflected in the disrupted affirmation of human rights which are in certain areas trampled under the pressure of the questionable political church groups whose main mission, which consists in their self-loving profiteering and upholding of their own positions, largely contributes to the entire disharmony of civil relations. Primarily, I wish to point out here the category of the so-called status differences which is the preliminary stumbling block for all other humanistic efforts. For, when a certain community is losing its own principles of equality and gains the contour of mutual differentiation on the grounds of ethnic, racial, and social differences, the life of double standards is born. One of those standards is the life belonging to the elite of rulers, i.e., the protagonists of the ethno-religious process, and their vassals who sustain this system. The other one is the life belonging to all other people who are, unfortunately, only the observers of the mentioned politicking religious movements.

This, in turn, gives rise to all sort of anomalies, pulling the people of a certain area deeper into the abyss of doubt, fear, and loathing. Or, as Moltmann would put it, it pulls them into the cruelty of the vicious circles, which, by their mutual actions, "bring the human life involved in them to a state of dehumanization and death."[12] In the first place, due to increasingly pronounced class differences, the degradation of humanity becomes apparent when a group of people within one and the same social group is considered less worthy than their wealthier and more powerful counterparts, since the category of belonging has become profitable and in some ways elevated above all other civilizational achievements,

---

11. Allusion to the book *The Lamb of God and the Beast from the Abyss* [*Jagnje Božije i Zvijer iz bezdana*], which, from the perspective of Serbian Orthodox Church, intends to justify the war in Bosnia and create a strong opposition to the antiwar movements in former Yugoslavia.

12. Moltmann, *Crucified God*, 332.

carefully wrapped up in precisely defined ideological procedures. This state of affairs, except through strictly *regime actions,* is also reflected through the actions of certain church officials, as this is, of course, a quite logical direction in the place where political religion reigns. It then follows that such a church, at a historical level, is primarily construed as the institution of the pro-regime spiritualistic foot soldiers, acting in a calculated manner exclusively for some private reasons, using the remaining part of the church as a nation, mainly for the purpose of statistical showing (proving) of numbers providing legitimacy to their social influence. Therefore, within the ethno-religious context, the *people of God* as members of Christ's community are not considered as equal participants of God's people by clergymen of a particular regime. They are rather manipulatively used as a percentage in the demonstration of power of the local political worship, with which, consequently, a great deal of that same percentage becomes more and more alienated in their belief in their dubious shepherds and their supporters, realizing to what extent the very politicking has corroded the contents of true worship.

> For priests, clericalism is a form of management stemming more from the governing power structures than from the service, thus always generating antagonisms between priests and the people.[13]

In this way, the institutional church steps into the sphere of spiritual schizophrenia or general division generated on account of its strict folklore hermetic tightness and the impossibility of a clear overview of the catastrophe of its institutional exclusiveness. This exclusiveness conforms to an almost concrete calling for social openness with the lunatic recalling of some of its mythologized past. The golden calves, the heroes of questionable historical credibility that are chosen amongst themselves, are often enthroned in this process. This kind of particularized church categorically may even belong under the aegis of the general Christian universality, but its way of behaving is definitely a perversion in relation to

13. Supičić, *Za univerzalni humanizam*, 343.

Christian fellowship, which unquestionably leads to the conclusion that it has become a mere sect of primarily local relevance, and deemed absolutely irrelevant for the mediation of God's universal plan for humanity. It is made irrelevant, considering that it is in this case utterly and completely determined by the will of clergy with their regime-like urges who insist on worshiping their own gods perceived in the image of their own nation, becoming in this way the protagonists of a *new paganism*. "We are faced with a new paganism: the deification of the nation."[14]

This model for the behavior of church officials leads to an inevitable alienation from the broader needs and concerns of the respective society. Politicized practice of acting within society had created an insensitive paradigm which becomes a home to the idolatry of idealized and narrow-minded ethnical cleanliness and its related customs. With this we might say that this kind of church, deeply within itself, has emotionally completely bypassed the memory of the sacrifice of Jesus Christ, i.e., his resistance towards elitism of the confessional practice of his time, delving deeper into the traumas of the time in which it was persecuted, inadvertently assuming the role of its own persecutors. But now, unconsciously, the church is trying to assign a completely different meaning to that same principle of oppression that it had previously rebuked, for the purpose of justifying its own actions.

> The failure of the religious institution—the Church—in my opinion, consists in the fact that it has distanced its own dogmatic memory of God from the memory of human suffering. Its invocation of the authority of God sometimes seems so fundamentalist, only because God's authority is moved away from the authority of the suffering ones.[15]

If this were not true, it would not be mainly characterized by the dispiritedness towards the spirit of contemporaneity. But instead of that, it defends itself from it so frantically, with the obsolete, safe religious postulates, in complete opposition to the faith

---

14. John Paul II, "Address," §7.
15. Metz, *Politička teologija*, 285.

of the Crucified One from which it originated in the first place. By abandoning its values in this way, it flies away from the Cross, away from the possibility of its own qualitative transformation, of a *rebirth*. In other words, by completely grounding the path of the church's own theological proclamation, it recognizes God as its Lord only until the beginning of his suffering, which is the last point that political religion can reach, since due to an immense self-loving urge it is unable to accept Christ's path of unconditional martyrdom solely as the product of pure divine love. Rather, the church often describes that path as the calculated pledge of a *social contract,* granting *mystical features to* a certain regime, whereby the church in return acquires the national territory as a polygon for the demonstration of ethno-religious ambitions.

Such an institutional church is still a sleepy player in the Garden of Gethsemane, who having slept through the crucial wake of his calling, startles and wakes up suddenly while instinctively pulling the sword from the sheaths and in utter misunderstanding of Christ's role. The institutional church uses the sword without hesitation, in a completely paradoxical move since that very blade is essentially directed against the intentions of God himself. Namely, if we consider that the Son's death has already been written—the holy death of soteriological feature—then the mentioned use of arms does not mean anything but resistance in narrow historical terms against the project of the kingdom of Heaven, where the executioners of Jesus of Nazareth undoubtedly play a part. Limited human understanding of divine truths can in no way serve as justification for that, primarily because the possibility of realization on the behalf of the institutional church has been missed out and any further attempt at explanation is a mere trivialization of that primeval religious feeling.

Political religion spins around in precisely this contradiction, while striving for the affirmation of its attitudes, and constantly startling itself from sleep, accidentally striking with its weapons on the fundaments of Christian teachings, creating in this way the chasm between uncontaminated religious desire for human progress and its own destructive practice of narrow politicking. This chasm between the religious desire and politicking also generates the ill-fated framework where secular society abides. I say ill-fated since, except for the pro-regime violation of human rights, there exists an entire opposite spectrum of possible social dialogue in which religion, with its own attitudes, supports humanistic actions within a certain area. However, since this is not the case within the discussed context, let us tackle the first issue, i.e., the polygon for ethno-religious manifestations as the definition of reality in which the majority of our social and theological movements exist.

At the social level, such usurpation of secular space becomes particularly obvious when church officials support ruling parties during state and national events as guests of honor and as distinguished participants in the mentioned manifestations. The same goes for the state officials who attend strictly religious ceremonies as major and distinguished participants of those events. Of course, this is not to say that priests cannot attend and celebrate state or national holidays, or vice versa, but what we challenge here is the underlying intention of their endeavours. Surely, no one in a society that aspires to democracy should forbid people to freely express their thoughts or beliefs, but surely we should challenge the actions of public officials so as to prevent, in this case, the accidental symbiosis of profane and sacral roles, where political religion exhibits its power, removing the boundaries between church and state while merging them into a single dominant and untouchable politicized entity which, untouched by the rest of the legal and political system, tries to take control over all aspects of life. "Faith becomes an important or even the sole factor of confirmation of mutual identity to the extent that stronger national or communal feelings can only be expressed in and through the religious 'second' language."[16] This is most evident in the relationship of the dominant political elites with church elites, who are given a sort of preferential treatment within the social frame in certain instances, for example in the sphere of justice, economy, or education.

Ethnoreligionism, with all the splendor of its vulgarized Christian expression, becomes entrenched in the orbit of the

16. Mardešić, *Lica i maske svetoga*, 285–86.

desires of individual private interests, forcing the institutional church to assume the role of the spiritual shepherd of the regime while resembling the one who upholds Christ's teachings only in outward religious appearances. Furthermore, having accepted the primacy of power structures, the church becomes the prisoner of worldly, materialistic desires and motives, which is clearly reflected in its frequent competition with the rest of the community regarding almost every issue, even the most trivial. Such trivialization of the mystical and divine character and its reduction to the common denominator of the vicissitudes of the system tramples any idea that this kind of religious lesson can have a positive social impact. Although its haughty stakeholders, the disputed clerical hierarchy, are eagerly trying to prove it—often with a very aggressive approach towards the pluralistic society of democratic aspirations—they do not realize that in this way they only plunge deeper into the slime of bigotry, obtuseness, and misunderstanding.

In this regard, a case in point is the position of religious education within the generally secular school curriculum, whereby the confession of faith is more often drilled than improved or upgraded, since political religion does not learn about itself from *the outside*, but exclusively presupposes about others from *the inside*. It presupposes that the entire world is precisely and only that which it represents itself to be, since its vision has grown out of an entirely endogenous *coalescence of religionism*, characterized by, I would say, a strict *folklore monotheism*, which sees God first as a foundation of ethnicity, and only then of religious expression. Or rather, this behavioral pattern of certain church circles has not so much denied the divine attributes to the Almighty as it has infiltrated and limited his actions to the strict area of the *folklore confession of faith*, on which the dimension of a local *Jerusalem* is repeatedly pinned. However, *Jerusalem* as such does not qualify as a living memory of the Crucified One as a foundation of a *new spiritual people*, but rather is a bulwark for the defense of an obsolete *Pharisaic pre-image*, while the memory of sacrifice does not generate the life-giving love of religious dynamism, but an *ethno-religious* prototype of the politicized lamentation over the killing fields of a nation.

In short, the birth, life, and death (including, if you will, the resurrection, as I will explain later) of God are perceived in strictly national frameworks, within which the memory and empathy are not directed towards all people, because there is a whole narrow-minded system which the *event of Jerusalem* strictly includes within the personal pseudo-historical memories, as the source of myriads of local mythical truths in the strict form of the conducted political worship. This takes us a few sentences back, because it unequivocally defines why political religion is not capable of learning from its surroundings. Rather, it can only impose on it its own personal attitudes, which consequently makes it considerably irrelevant within today's social dialogue. And if we are to add to this a certain oxymoron in the sense that the pro-regime clergy does not always particularly support the discussed ethnic and religious fundamentalism out of their own personal attitudes, but rather out of the fact that it has become their only frame of existence, then we will become aware of the full weakness of that seemingly monumental system.

Therefore, we may conclude that this radical form of political servitude is in some way a self-destructive existence which would not be questionable on a wider humanistic plane if such a suicidal process had no effect on other religious and secular affairs. Since every initiative within the denominational, ecumenical, interreligious, and social dialogue is entirely thwarted by individuals who fight bitterly to preserve their own thrones, it turned them into a strong material surrogate of their conspicuous moral decay.

In short, *ethno-religionism* exists in the unconscious trauma of the fear of one's own calling, in which only a good God can be the one who was violently crucified, because this indirectly allows the possibility of building strong, *religious,* emotional blackmail on the basis of God's passion, and above all his grave, equally applicable to all particular historical frameworks. Jesus's voluntary journey to Golgotha opens up a number of rhetorical questions for the clergy, preventing them from making any counterarguments as they are ultimately disclosed by Jesus as the long arm of the former executioners of God. It is this pathology that the secular community intensively feels, because it has become the object upon which the political religion is trying to transfer the feeling of guilt for their own wrongdoings, and in this way to impose a radical form of forced repentance on society, thus bringing it to the altar of political worship, which uses liturgy only as an extension of the war by other means.

This attempt to transfer the guilt and its consecration to the altar particularly comes to the fore in the intense and overbearing campaign of the politicized priests against the atheistic stance of some citizens, who are incessantly demonized and are ascribed actions of apocalyptical social scale. This hyping up of a dangerous atmosphere by turning mere opponents into arch enemies is quite typical of *ethno-religious* rhetoric, which clearly suggests that the political religion can only exist if it is faced with threats, even fabricated ones. The reason for this is, of course, that this kind of *folklorized* faith finds no footing in Christian teaching, due to its intolerance to non-God and its need for some other legitimizing justification, fulfilled through the phantasm of the *threatening other, the only one who can at the same time be* the point of reference for its real existence.

This means, finally, that the ethno-religious wraith is only alive and effective when it is born out of a masochistic process, in which it aspires to its own death at the hand of whichever enemy in order to give physical features to its self-imposed metaphysical suffering. This leads to the laconic conclusion that political worship arguably considers a Pharisaic death sentence to be more important than the healing grace of God, because it does not draw its strength from the event of Christ's resurrection, but from the darkest part of the tomb of Jesus of Nazareth.

THE AUTOPSY OF THE ETHNO-RELIGIOUS POLITICAL WORSHIP

In order to be functional, the ethno-religious version of political worship must be killed incessantly since its life does not originate from the living human effort, but from the dead bodies of carefully defined hardships, due to its incapability to be guided by the teachings of the Living God. It defends itself by the silence of graves dug long ago. This is where a major issue arises in the attempt to unveil and demystify this confessional concept. Namely, unlike most other similar cases, the socio-theological methodology will not suffice here, as one further step needs to be made beyond the social movements which applies something that could be characterized as a *theological autopsy*. However, this should not be surprising considering that the actual political religion is mainly represented as the religion of yearning for death, and not for life, whose foothold is deeply buried in the *ideology of killing fields* wherein on a historical level it appears solely as a wraith trying to ascertain some *afterlife rules* of mythological features in the contemporary society of humanist tendencies.

It is for this reason that we need a *theological autopsy* whose worldly efforts will go so far as to carry out exhumations on all *ethno-religiously anointed* burial grounds until it ascertains that there is nothing historically grounded save the vanity and greed of the individuals who use the genuine victims of a certain time period for their own personal benefit. This could, possibly, indirectly affect the general doctrine of political worship, superciliously residing for centuries now at the bottom of the crypt of Jesus of Nazareth, frozen in the image of suffering, rage, and bitterness while, graphically presented, never reaching the next historical frame which is the event of resurrection, an event representing the *deus ex machina* that finally puts an end to it.

For that reason, the political religion is unable to truly grasp either the modus of the *theology of the cross*, since it is entirely defined by the acute form of its expression manifested through a peculiar facet of the presented quasi-theological concept or the *necrophilia of religionism*. Consequently, as already pointed out several times before, its relevance to the contemporary civilization developments is lost since its humanistic evolution has stopped exactly where all other originated. Today, this can be very well perceived in the actions and behavior of its followers who could be named *pseudo-apostolic narcoleptics* based on the ancient events in the Garden of Gethsemane, whose personality finds its primary source in self-confident but heretic serving, because having deliriously misunderstood their own faith, they have caused a series of social disagreements in their frantic insistence on some acquired functions. Namely, they have stripped themselves of any spec of humanity unbecoming to their governing duty within the politicized worshiping in order to become an authentic paragons of the ideology founded on the noncritical symbiosis of strictly defined nation and strictly defined confession of faith, thus spawning *the ethno-religious wraith* of entirely dubious social givens.

This shallow form of existence of the so-called office seekers constitutes a dangerous break with a life-giving work of God, and completely sidelines the present work of the spirit in affirmation of its own "functionalized" role and its ideological roots. In this way, they appear as mere wreckages and caricatures of discipleship—as meaningless corpses of what was once a living spirit of faith. And when a *dead body* carries a *dead faith* by means of dead political and religious concept, then it becomes perfectly clear why it turns into a wraith which stands in complete opposition to the Christianity as a religion of the Living God, notwithstanding the fact that it appeals to the very heart of its teachings, taking it only as a *masquerade mask* to conceal their politicized actions. "When covered with a mask of holiness, politics is better sheltered and thus more successful in manipulating the true religious feelings and values."[17]

This further leads to the conclusion that the institutional church in the service of political worshiping is in principle ecclesial heresy defined by, I would name it, a *voluntary blasphemy*, i.e., the church in its role of a regime caretaker is distancing itself from the

---

17. Ibid., 285.

classless God of the call of the Gospel, and in this dispirited heat of passion which is caracterized by its strong tyrannical and selfish features attacks both the very foundations of Christian teaching and the humanistic process of social maturation.

> Faith is fearful and defensive when it begins to die inwardly, struggling to maintain itself and reaching out for security and guarantees. In so doing, it removes itself from the hand of the one who has promised to maintain it, and its own manipulations bring it to ruin.[18]

Roughly speaking, this current of aggressive hermetical clericalism, instead of worshiping places, engenders new sites of slaughter undisputedly emanating all its perfidious rhetoric which easily contaminates the life of a nation with the elements intended at social turmoil. This happens as the passion of their action is inversely proportional to the humanization of social processes, because the more the implementation of human rights as well as the effectiveness of the legal system is thwarted, the louder the pro-regime voices within certain Churh groups are. Their posthumous march leads the life beyond the river Styx, into its natural habitat of afterlife existence in which all values of worldly existence are distorted, and where religionism replaces religion and politicking replaces politics, creating an extremely fertile ground for the rise of the ethno-religious wraith, which does not see this form of existence as its end, but quite the contrary, it turns the tomb of humanity into a cradle of its own birth.

This newborn eerie spawn of civilization pulls the world into a clerical dusk zone which is in clear confrontation with the society of a true Christian faith and humanistic secular aspirations, because it does not adhere to the ethical postulates of its Teacher, but rather using a *quasi-theology of subsequent martyrdom*. This is that sort of the pro-regime-programmed memory that adopts fabrication as a branch of history and artily overemphasizes the sufferings of the right kind of victims adorning them with garlands and processions in the symbolism of its own private interests.

---

18. Moltmann, *Crucified God*, 29.

Turning of the killing fields and graves into the trophies of politicking worshiping is, in certain sense, a death proclaimed to the living, as if political religion seems to say that only *dead* believers can be good believers, all the while of course taking their national features into consideration; namely, believers uncritically accept the form of political worshiping while stripping themselves of the primordial religious and faith content. Such coarse trivialization of national sufferings, thrown into the machinery for manufacturing of the *folklore confession of faith* is a clear indication of an urgent need of a theological *autopsy*. In other words, a careful dissection of political worshiping would reveal all the anomalies of this impaired system and allow us to prevent it from further feeding on the dead. It opens up a possibility of heralding the beginning of the end of ethno-religionism, gradually liberating the entire institutional church from the giant wraith of regime. At the same time, they give the contemporary society space for the development and growth in the dialogue of the concrete sacred and concrete secular views, without still omnipresent masked hypocrisy. In short, instead of masquerading, they should be restoring the deposit of faith (*depositum fidei*).[19]

---

19. In this sentence a pun is made with similar sounding words for *masquerade* and *deposit* in the Croatian language—*poklade*, and *poklad* respectively [translator's note].

BIBLIOGRAPHY

Buden, Boris. *Barikade 2*. Zagreb: Arkzin, 1996.
Guénon, René. *The Crisis of the Modern World*. Translated by Arthur Osborne et al. 4th rev. ed. Collected Works of René Guénon. Ghent, NY: Sophia Perennis, 2001.
Gutiérrez, Gustavo. *A Theology of Liberation: History, Politics and Salvation*. Translated and edited by Sister Caridad Inda and John Eagleson. London: SCM, 1974.
Kiš, Danilo. *A Tomb for Boris Davidovich*. Translated by Duska Mikic-Mitchell. London: Faber, 1985.
John Paul II. "Address of His Holiness John Paul II to the Diplomatic Corps Accredited to the Holy See." Vatican, January 15, 1994. https://w2.vatican.va/content/john-paul-ii/en/speeches/1994/january/documents/hf_jp-ii_spe_19940115_corpo-diplomatico.html.
Mardešić, Željko. *Lica i maske svetoga*. Zagreb: Kršćanska sadašnjost, 1997.
Metz, Johannes Baptist. *Politička teologija*. Translated by Željko Čekolj. Zagreb: Kršćanska sadašnjost, 2004.
Mladenović, Radoš M., and Jeromonah Jovan Ćulibrk, eds. *Jagnje Božije i Zvijer iz bezdana: Filosofija rata*. Cetinje, Svetigora: Izdavačka ustanova Mitropolije Crnogorsko-primorske, 1996.
Moltmann, Jürgen. *The Crucified God: The Cross of Christ as the Foundation and Criticism of Christian Theology*. Translated by R. A. Wilson and John Bowden. Minneapolis: Fortress, 1993.
Roksandić, Drago. "Religious Tolerance and Division in the Krajina: The Croatian Serbs of the Habsburg Military Border." In *Christianity and Islam in Southeastern Europe*, 49–82. Washington, DC: Woodrow Wilson Center for East European Studies, 1997.
Šarčević, Ivan. "Politička religija." *Svjetlo riječi* (2011) 340–41.
Supičić, Ivan. *Za univerzalni humanizam: Prema potpunijoj čovječnosti*. Zagreb: Kršćanska sadašnjost, 2010.
Vrcan, Srđan. "Religija i politika—Simptomatični primjer bivše Jugoslavije devedesetih godina 20. stoljeća." *Glasilo građanskog samooslobađanja. Republika* (2003) 320–21.

Index

Adorno, Th. W., 23, 29, 34, 35, 39, 65
Ahn-Byun-Mu, 16
Almond, G., 57

Balthasar, H. U. von xix, 88, 99–103, 104–8
Barth, K., 12
Bauckham, R., 9, 10
Beiser, F., 27
Bloch, E., 7, 22, 26, 39
Bonhoeffer, D., 35, 36, 51, 75, 83, 94
Brandt, W., 9
Brenkert, G., 57
Buber, M., 5
Bucher, R., 75, 76
Buden, B., 125
Bultmann, R., 12

Celan, P., 3
Chagall, M., 2
Cone, J., 15, 16
Cox, H., 6

Dahrendorf, R., 56
Dogan, N., 22
Dotolo, C., 72
Dubček, A., 7
Dutschke, R., 7

Đogo, D., 20

Elazar, D. J., 57
Ellacuría, I., 13
Garaudy, R., 7
Gardavsky, V., 8
Gibson, J., 56
Guénon, R., 124
Gutiérrez, G., 11, 12, 118

Habermas, J., 55
Hegel, G. W. F., 23, 25–29, 32, 33, 36, 37, 40, 41, 108
Heidegger, M., 72, 76
Henrich, D., 27
Herzog, F., 14
Hölderlin, F., 59
Horkheimer, M., 23, 39
John Paul II, pope, 10, 11, 128
John XXIII, pope, 8
Jüngel, E., 25, 28

Kant, I., 27
Karlić, I., 22
Käsemann, Elisabeth, 12, 13
Käsemann, Ernst, 12
Kohl, H., 5
Küng, H., 29, 55

Lochmann, J. M., 39
Loewenich, W. von, 31
Lohse, B., 31
Luther, M., 15, 23, 26, 27, 29, 30, 31, 32, 33, 37, 40, 97

Index

Luther King, M., 6

Machovec, M., 7, 8
Mardešić, Ž., 59, 79, 80, 82, 130
Marsch, W.-D., 6, 26
Marx, K., 12, 22
Máté-Tóth, A., 58
Mateljan, A., 22
Matić, M., 22
McAfee Brown, R., 13
Metz, J. B. xix, 7, 14, 24, 25, 34, 65, 89, 93, 110, 113, 128
Migliore, D., 39
Miguez-Bonino, J., 12
Miskotte, H. H., 39

Nietzsche, F., 25, 28, 32, 36, 72, 110
Nohl, H., 27

Ohnesorg, B., 7

Pavić, Ž., 47
Pehar, M., 22
Pitstick, A. L., 101, 104–7, 109, 114
Prucha, M., 8

Queiruga, A. T., 60

Rahner, K., 7, 75, 83
Ratzinger, J., 9, 55, 123, 124
Rouet, A., 81, 82

Sander, H. J., 81
Schelling, F. W. J., 27
Sobrino, J. xvii, 13, 70
Sölle, D., 34
Somoza, A., 13
Sremac, S., 20, 114
Supičić, I., 127

Šarčević, I., 20, 65, 96, 122
Škvorčević, A., 22

Vattimo, G. xviii, 47, 51, 72, 74, 75, 76
Verba, S., 57
Volf, M. xiii, 56
Vrcan, S., 125

Welker, M., 1, 32, 33, 39
Wiesel, W., 5, 24, 35
Wildavsky, A., 57
Žižek, S., 77

www.ingramcontent.com/pod-product-compliance
Lightning Source LLC
Chambersburg PA
CBHW022122160426
43197CB00009B/1120